Ages 9+

101

SCIENCE
EXPERIMENTS
and projects

This book belongs to

_____

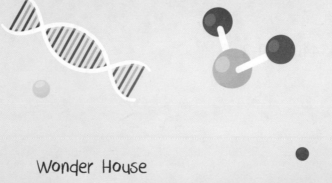

Wonder House

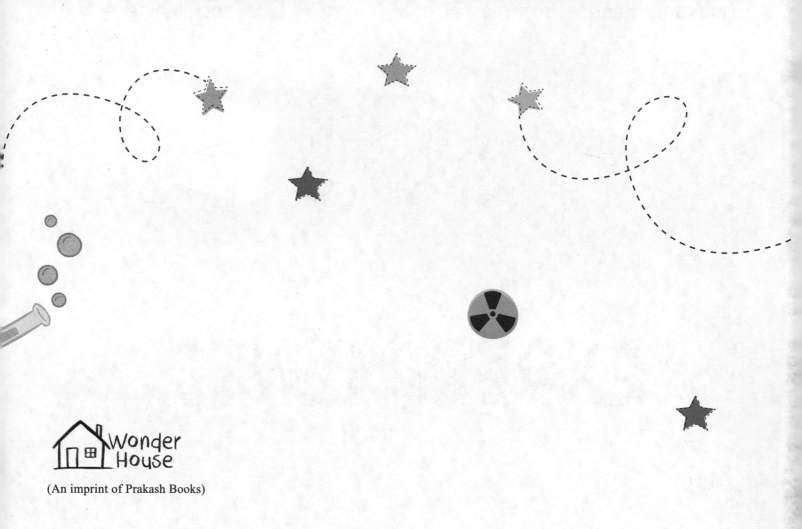

Wonder House

(An imprint of Prakash Books)

contact@wonderhousebooks.com

ISBN : 978-93-54402-30-2

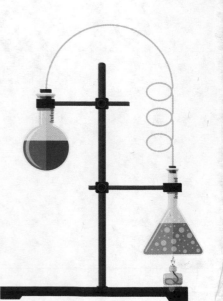

Contents

EXPERIMENTS WITH

AIR & GASES

Air is all around us though we cannot see it. It is not only important for our survival but also helps us in many other ways, such as for burning fuel, blowing balloons, flying aircrafts, and making things work.

Air is a mixture of gases with traces of water vapor and other substances. It has specific properties.

Air has mass.
_____
Air exerts pressure and has weight.
_____
Air occupies space.

Air can be compressed.
_____
Temperature impacts air.

1

STAB A POTATO

Life Connect: Air pressure

You Need
- A raw potato
- A drinking straw

1

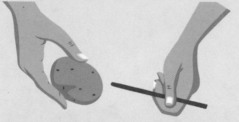

Hold the potato firmly in one hand. Now, hold the straw by its sides in the other hand. Do not cover the hole at the top of the straw.

2

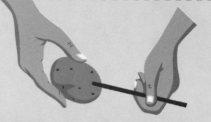

Try to stab the potato. Does the straw pierce through the potato? No, it bends.

3

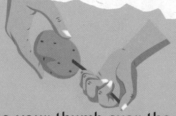

Now, place your thumb over the hole at the top of the straw. Hold the potato from one end and push the straw into the potato.

4

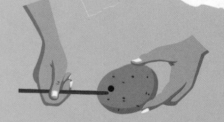

This time, the straw pierces deep into the potato.

The STEM behind it

Placing your thumb over the hole captures the air inside the straw.

Air is compressed and pushes out against the straw. Hence, the straw becomes rigid and strong enough to pierce through the potato!

2

CRUSH A CAN

Life Connect: Air pressure

DIFFICULTY LEVEL

Adult supervision required

1 Take an empty soda can. Pour approximately 20-30 ml of water into it.

2 Next, fill a large bowl with cold water and ice.

3 Have an adult heat the can on the stove until the water inside the can comes to a boil. Make sure the can is upright while heating it.

4 Now, turn the hot can upside down into the bowl of cold water and ice. Step aside.

The can crushes quickly with a loud noise!

The STEM behind it

When the water inside the can comes to a boil, it escapes in the form of steam into the air. It also pushes air out of the can.

When we place the can in cold water and ice, the water vapor inside it cools down rapidly creating a vacuum. The pressure inside the can is now lower than outside.

The air on the outside pushes the can hard causing it to crush.

BALLOON CAR

DIFFICULTY LEVEL

Life Connect: Jet engines

You Need
- Cardboard
- Utility knife
- Scissors
- 2 straws
- Tape
- Wooden skewers or lollipop sticks
- 4 equal bottle caps
- A balloon

1 Draw a 3 by 6 inch rectangle on the cardboard using a pen or pencil. Then, cut it using a pair of scissors or a utility knife.

2 Take a straw and cut two 3 inch pieces from it. Do not include the bendy part of the straw.

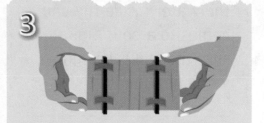

3 Lay the pieces of straw on the cardboard and secure them with tape. Fix them firmly.

4 Using a utility knife, cut two 4 inch pieces from the wooden skewer.

5 Push the pieces of skewer through the straws such that about ½ inch of each piece sticks out of the straws.

6 With the help of an adult, poke a hole in the centre of each bottle cap.

7 Fix the bottle caps at the ends of the wooden skewers, as shown.

8 Take a balloon and tape its neck tightly around one end of the straw.

9

Turn the car upside down and make it stand on the caps (i.e. its wheels.) Tape the straw and the balloon onto the cardboard such that the balloon rests on top of the cardboard and some part of the straw hangs over one of its ends.

10

Blow through the straw and inflate the balloon. Carefully place your finger over the tip of the straw. Place the car on a flat, smooth surface and then remove your finger. Watch your car zoom around in the room.

The STEM behind it

The elastic material of the balloon has potential energy stored in it. When we blow air inside the balloon more potential energy is added to it (because the air is at rest inside the balloon).

When we remove our finger from the straw, the potential energy inside the balloon changes to kinetic energy.

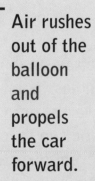

Air rushes out of the balloon and propels the car forward.

WIND VANE

DIFFICULTY LEVEL

Life Connect: Studying weather patterns

1

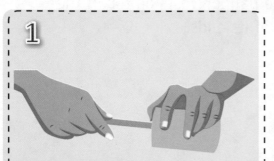

Make a hole in the middle of a plastic can using a pencil. Push the sharp end of the pencil through the hole.

2

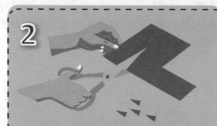

Then draw two large triangles and four small triangles on a colored sheet and cut them out using scissors.

3

Glue the small triangles (pointing outwards) onto the plastic cup in four different directions, as shown in the picture.

4

Take a straw and cut short slits on both its ends. Insert the large triangles into each end of the straw such that one end has a pointed triangle end and the other has the base. The vane is ready.

5

With the help of an adult, push a board pin through the centre of the straw. Carefully push the set up into the eraser on the pencil.

6 Take modeling clay and make a ring out of it. The ring should be a little larger than the mouth of the plastic pot.

7 Push the plastic pot firmly on the ring so that it does not blow away.

8 Mount the wind vane outside on an elevated shaft. With the help of a compass, position it such that the small triangles point north, south, east and west as shown in the picture. The vane rotates in the direction of the wind.

The STEM behind it

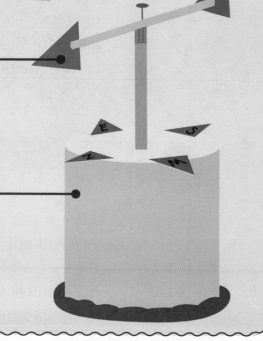

The vane is made such that it allows movement about a vertical axis. Both the ends of the vane have equal weight, which allows the vane to rotate freely.

The arrow always points in the direction from where wind is blowing.

The directional markers allow us to identify the direction easily.

5
EGG IN A BOTTLE

Life Connect: Difference in air pressure on heating

1 Peel the shell off the boiled egg when it is cool enough to handle.

You Need
- A hard-boiled egg
- A jar or bottle (with a mouth slightly smaller than the width of an egg)
- A strip of paper (approximately 8x1-inch)
- A lighter

2 Place the egg at the mouth of the bottle. As expected, it does not slide into the bottle.

3 With the help of an adult, light one end of a paper strip and place it inside the bottle.

4 Immediately place the egg back at the mouth of the bottle before the paper burns out.

5 After a few seconds, you will notice that the egg wiggles a little and squeezes down into the bottle.

The STEM behind it

The burning paper inside the bottle heats up the air around it.

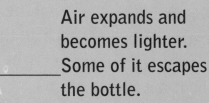

Air expands and becomes lighter. Some of it escapes the bottle.

When the paper burns out, the air inside the bottle cools and contracts. The air pressure inside the bottle is less than the air pressure outside. The air outside the bottle (high-pressure area) tries to flow into the bottle (low-pressure area) and, in process, pushes the egg into the bottle!

6
AIR TAKES UP SPACE

Life Connect: Blowing balloons and footballs

DIFFICULTY LEVEL

You Need
- A bottle
- Modeling clay
- A funnel
- Water

1  Place the funnel into the mouth of a bottle and pour some water into it. What happens? The water flows into the bottle.

2  Now, remove the funnel from the bottle.

3 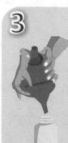 Wrap modeling clay around the funnel and carefully seal the space between the funnel and the bottle.

4  Secure the funnel to the bottle. Smooth out the clay with your fingers such that the space between the funnel and the bottle is airtight.

5  Pour water into the funnel. The water just stays in the funnel and does not flow into the bottle.

The STEM behind it

 Water cannot flow into the bottle as air takes up space inside.

Air cannot escape from the bottle as the space between the funnel and the bottle is sealed with clay.

If we pour water slowly, some water flows into the bottle because there is enough room in the opening of the funnel for both water and air. However, if we pour water very quickly, only a small amount of water flows into the bottle. This is because the opening of the funnel fills with water, which blocks the flow of air and remains in the funnel!

DRY ICE SMOKE RING LAUNCHER

Life Connect: Artifical fog effects

DIFFICULTY LEVEL

You Need
- A coin
- Plastic cup
- Scissors or utility knife
- A pen
- A thick plastic bag
- Rubber bands
- Warm water
- Dry ice
- Heavy gloves

 1 Turn the cup upside down. Place a coin at the center and trace it using a pen.

2 Use a utility knife to cut out the traced circle.

 **3** Place a plastic bag over the open end of the cup and secure it using a rubber band.

 4  Trim away the extra plastic using scissors.

5  Pour 60 ml of warm water into the cup through the hole at the cup's bottom.

6   Wear gloves and carefully drop 2 pieces of dry ice into the hole. The pieces should be small enough to fit through the hole.

7  After a few seconds, you will notice white vapors belching out of the hole.

8  Now, hold the cup with one hand such that the plastic wrap faces you. Tilt the cup and tap the plastic layer. White rings shoot out in no time!

The STEM behind it

Dry ice is frozen carbon dioxide. When we drop a piece of dry ice into warm water, the water's heat raises the temperature of the ice, changing it into gas (CO_2).

The CO_2 coming out of the cup cools the water vapor in the air. The white rings are a combination of carbon dioxide and water vapour.

Air escaping the cup through the center of the hole travels faster than the air leaving from around the edges of the hole. This difference in speed creates a swirling motion, which appears in the form of rings in the air.

8
MAKE A BALLOON ROCKET

DIFFICULTY LEVEL

Life Connect: Launching a rocket

You Need
- A piece of string about 2 m long
- 2 chairs
- A drinking straw
- A balloon
- Masking tape

1 Position both the chairs about 10 ft apart. Then, securely tie one end of the string to one of the chairs.

2 Lace the string through the drinking straw.

3 Tie the other end of the string to the second chair. Make sure the string is stretched tight.

4 Blow up a balloon and hold its neck so that no air escapes.

5 Using two pieces of tape, secure the balloon to the straw. Keep the neck of the balloon closed as you tape it to the straw.

6 Move the straw and the balloon to one end of the string. Now, let go of the balloon The balloon will take the straw to the other chair.

The STEM behind it

This experiment is a simple example of how a rocket engine works.

Action: The elastic skin of the balloon puts pressure on the air inside the balloon.

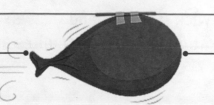

Reaction: When we released the balloon, the air rushed out of the open-end causing the balloon to move (in the opposite direction).

MAGIC CANDLE FLAME

DIFFICULTY LEVEL

You Need
- A candle
- A lighter

Life Connect: Air pressure

1 Place a candle on a flat surface and light it using a lighter.

2 Blow out the candle with a short breath and wait for a few seconds. You should see a trail of smoke rising from the candle's wick.

3 Bring the lighter close to the smoke coming from the wick and place the flame. Make sure not to touch the wick. The candle lights once again!

The STEM behind it

When we light the candle, the wax close to the wick melts, turning into liquid. This melted wax travels up the wick. Here, it gets hotter, turns into a gas and evaporates.

When we blow out the candle, the wick stays hot and the wax continues to evaporate. On placing the flame near the wick, the wax vapor reignites and the flame travels to the wick, lighting the candle again.

10
DO NOT FALL

Life Connect: Air pressure

You Need
- A clear drinking glass
- A thin flat card
- Water

1 Fill a clear drinking glass to the top with water.

2 Place a flat card on the glass such that it completely covers its mouth.

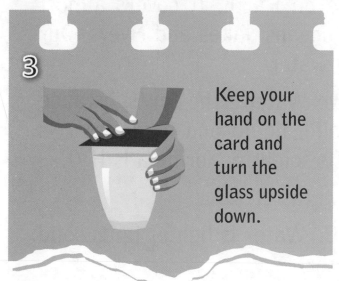

3 Keep your hand on the card and turn the glass upside down.

4 Slowly take your hand away. The card and the water still stay in place!

The STEM behind it

When we turn the glass upside down, very little water leaks out of it. The volume of air above the water increases but the air pressure decreases.

The pressure outside the glass is now greater than inside the glass. This keeps the card in place and prevents water from falling.

EXPERIMENTS WITH

WATER & OTHER LIQUIDS

Water plays a very important role on Earth. It covers almost 75% of our planet in the form of oceans, lakes and rivers. Our body is also made up of 60 to 70% water.

All living things need water to survive. Water is the only substance that occurs in all three states—solid, liquid and gas. Water is made up of hydrogen and oxygen. Its scientific formula is H_2O.

Pure water is colorless, odorless and tasteless.

It boils at 100°C and freezes at 0°C. Water is lighter in its solid state (ice) than its liquid state (water).

Water is called a universal solvent because it dissolves most of the substances.

Water is not only used for drinking and to do other household chores but also to generate electricity.

FLOATING ORANGE

Life Connect: How things float and sink?

DIFFICULTY LEVEL

You Need
- Two oranges
- Two tall clear jugs
- Water

1 Fill both the jugs 3/4th with water. Slowly place an orange into one of the jugs. The orange will float.

2 Next, remove the peel from the second orange.

3 Carefully put the peeled orange into the second jug. This time the orange sinks. What just happened?

The STEM behind it

When the peeled orange is submerged in water, it pushes down and displaces water according to its weight. Also, the water pushes the orange up with a force equal to the weight of the water it displaces. This is called buoyancy.

The orange rind is very porous and is filled with tiny air pockets. The air pockets increase buoyancy and make the orange less dense than water, making it float.

Removing the rind of the orange makes it denser than water. Hence, it sinks.

12
DEEP-SEA DIVER

Life Connect: Working of submarines

You Need
- 2 ltr empty plastic bottle
- Play-dough
- A plastic pen cap

1

Roll some play-dough into a small ball and stick it to the bottom of a pen cap. This is your toy diver.

2

Fill a bottle to brim with water and place the toy diver in it. Close the bottle and tighten the cap.

3

Gently squeeze the bottle from the middle with both hands. Your toy diver sinks to the bottom.

4
Release your hands and the toy diver rises to the top!

The STEM behind it

When the pen cap is placed in the bottle full of water, a bubble of air is trapped inside it which makes it float.

When we squeeze the sides of the bottle, water enters the pen cap and the bubble of air gets smaller, which makes the cap sink to the bottom. Releasing the grip again makes the air bubble bigger, making the cap float once more.

MAKE YOUR DRAWINGS FLOAT

Life Connect: Hydrothermal

DIFFICULTY LEVEL

You Need
- A shallow ceramic plate
- Dry-erase marker
- Water

1 Take a ceramic plate and draw anything you like using the dry-erase marker.

2 Let it dry for a few minutes.

3 Slowly pour water into the plate close to the edges of the drawing. Wait and observe.

4 Your drawing starts to lift off the plate and floats on the surface of water!

The STEM behind it

The ink of the dry-erase marker contains oily silicone polymer which prevents our drawing from sticking to the plate. Also, the density of this ink is less than water.

When we pour water into the plate, the drawing is not washed away because the ink is insoluble in water.

A strong buoyant force magically detaches the drawing from the plate. The ink being lighter than water makes the drawing float on the surface.

TOUCH A BUBBLE

DIFFICULTY LEVEL

Life Connect: Why do bubbles burst?

1 Take warm water in a glass and add 1 tablespoon of glycerine to it.

2  Then, add approximately 1 tablespoon of dish soap to the glass.

3  Slowly stir the solution until it is mixed properly. Try not to form foam while stirring.

4  Ask a friend to put on a woolen glove.

5  Dip the bubble wand into the mixture and slowly pull it out.

6  Blow the bubbles. Ask your friend to take a bubble in her hand. The bubble won't burst for quite some time!

The STEM behind it

The outside of a bubble is made up of three very thin layers: soap, water and another layer of soap.

Glycerine makes the wall of the bubble denser and stronger, preventing it from bursting immediately.

The woolen glove reduces the area of contact of the bubble.

15
FIREWORKS IN A GLASS

Life Connect: Density and insoluble liquids

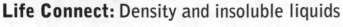

DIFFICULTY LEVEL

You Need
- A tall glass or jug
- Water
- Vegetable oil
- Food coloring

1

Take a tall glass or jug and fill it half with water.

2

Carefully pour some vegetable oil into the jug. You will observe that the oil will float above the water.

3

Slowly pour the food coloring above the oil. You may use two to three colors of your choice.

4

The food coloring droplets initially drop through the oil and form beads at the boundary between the layer of oil and water.

5

The droplets of food coloring slowly break through the water and spread out as they stream downwards towards the bottom of the glass.

6

The food coloring beads will continue to drop out of the oil and look like fireworks in a glass.

The STEM behind it

Food coloring is denser than water so it sinks down, leaving trails that resemble little fireworks.

The density of oil is less than water. Also, oil does not mix with water. Both these factors make oil float on the surface of water in the jug.

26

16
POWER YOUR BOAT WITH SOAP

Life Connect: Surface Tension

DIFFICULTY LEVEL
○ ○ ○ ○ ○

You Need
- Cardboard or thick paper
- Pencil
- Black marker
- A tub of water
- A pair of scissors
- Glue
- Liquid detergent or soap

1

Draw a boat shape on a cardboard or thick paper.

2

Then, make a small notch at the back of the boat in the middle of the rear edge. This is your target point.

3

Cut out the picture of the boat along the outlines. This makes our boat.

4

Gently, place the boat into the tub of water.

5

Squeeze a drop of detergent, or soap, onto the notch of the boat.

6

The boat races forward across the tub.

The STEM behind it

Soap reduces the surface tension of water around the rear end of the boat.

The surface tension pulling at the front of the boat is now greater than the force pulling at it from behind, so the boat moves forward. This is known as the Marangoni Effect.

UNDERWATER VOLCANO

Life Connect: Surface Tension

DIFFICULTY LEVEL

You Need
- A small clear glass bottle
- A pair of scissors
- A large glass jar (taller than the bottle)
- String
- Food coloring
- Hot and cold water

1

Cut a long piece of string and tie one of its ends firmly into a knot around the neck of a small bottle.

2

Thread the other end and do the same in the opposite direction of the first knot.
Ensure that the knots are tight. This is your handle to pick the bottle.

3

Next, take the large glass jar and fill it 3/4th with cold water.

4

With the help of an adult, fill the small bottle with hot water.
Add red food coloring to it so that the water turns red.

5

Carefully pick up the bottle by the string loop and lower it gently into the jar of cold water.

6

The hot red water begins to rise out of the bottle just like smoke and lava from an erupting volcano.

The STEM behind it

Hot water is less dense than cold water. When we place the hot water bottle into the jar of cold water, the hot water rises to the top of the container. It circulates at the top of the container, which looks like an erupting volcano.

Liquids with less density rise and those with more density sink.

18
MAGIC SAND

DIFFICULTY LEVEL

Adult supervision required

Life Connect: Hydrophobic substances

You Need
- Colored sand
- A large jar of water
- A shallow container or tray
- Fabric protector spray
- Wax paper or tin foil
- A spoon

1
Line the shallow container or tray with wax paper or tin foil.

Spread the colored sand onto it. Then, spray fabric protector onto the sand. After a few minutes, stir the sand and spray another coat of fabric protector onto it. You may use as many colors as you want and prepare different trays.
2

3
Let the sand dry for about an hour.

4
Keep the colored sand in different containers. Fill a jar with water.

5
Now, pour the colored sand into the jar of water.

6
The sand clumps together at the bottom of the jar.

7
Pull some sand out of the water. You will observe that it is completely dry and loose. When you drop it back into the water, it would clump back together again.

The STEM behind it

The fabric protector contains organofluorine chemicals and petroleum distillates. When the protector is sprayed onto the sand, its surface is exposed to a special chemical treatment. This makes the sand hydrophobic i.e. 'water-fearing'. It repels water and looks clumpy.

WHY DOES WATER RISE?

DIFFICULTY LEVEL

Adult supervision required

Life Connect: Effects of hot and cool air

1

Add 2-3 drops of food coloring to the water and mix it well so that the color dissolves completely in it.

2

Pour the colored water into a plate.

3

Set a candle in the center of the plate. Place the slender container over the candle and into the water. Check if its base is well above the candle wick and its top edge is submerged under the water.

4

Once the candle is stable on the plate and the water is still, light the candle. Let the candle flame burn brightly.

5

Carefully, turn the container and lower it over the burning candle. Place it on the plate in the water as shown.

6

You might see bubbles coming from inside the container. Water rises in the container and the candle keeps burning. After some time, the candle goes out and the water rises quickly in the container.

The STEM behind it

The candle flame heats the air inside the container which expands quickly. Some of this hot expanding air escapes from under the container.

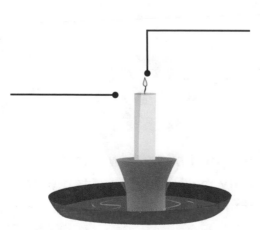

When the flame fades and goes out, the air in the container cools and contracts. This creates a weak vacuum or a lower pressure in the container.

The air from outside presses down on the water in the dish and pushes it into the container until the pressure is equalized both inside and outside the container.

20
WALKING WATER

Life Connect: Transportation in plants

You Need
- 7 identical glass jars
- Red, yellow, blue and green food coloring
- Water
- Paper towels

1

Fill four glass jars 3/4th with water. Leave the other three jars empty.

2

Add a few drops of red food coloring to the first jar of water, yellow to the second, green to the third and blue to the fourth jar. Mix the colors evenly in each jar.

3

Take a strip of paper towel and fold it in half such that it is about 2 inches wide. Repeat the same with six other paper towels.

4

Now prepare the setup. Place the 7 jars as shown.

5

Next, take the paper towels. Dip one end of a paper towel into the first jar with colored water. Place the other end into the empty jar. Repeat the step with other paper towels and jars. Leave the jars alone for an hour.

6

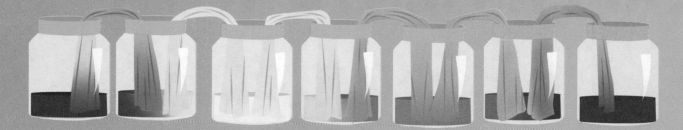

After sometime you will see that the water has traveled up the paper towels from the jars with colored water to the empty jars, and the colors have gotten mixed together.

The STEM behind it

Capillary action and attractive forces make the water 'walk'. Capillary action is the ability of a liquid to travel upwards against gravity.
The paper towels acted like capillary tubes to transport water. Paper towels are made of cellulose fibers and water flows upwards through tiny gaps between these fibers.

The attractive force between the paper towel and water is stronger which makes water defy gravity and travel across the paper towel out of one jar into another.

EXPERIMENTS WITH

HEAT

Heat is defined as the degree of hotness or coldness of an object. It is an essential form of energy that is used for various activities such as cooking, heating things, ironing, manufacturing of glass, paper and textiles and to run rail engines.

Heat is always transferred from a warmer to a colder body or area. It takes place through three modes—conduction, convection and radiation.

CONDUCTING HEAT

Life Connect: Heat transfer in solids

DIFFICULTY LEVEL

1 Take a glass bowl. Position the spoons in it such that their handles are down and their upper portion lies comfortably out of the bowl.

2 Pat some butter at the top of each spoon using a spatula.

3 Carefully place a bead on the pat of butter in each spoon.

4 With the help of an adult, pour boiling water into the bowl upto the brim. Be careful that the spoons remain in the same position.

5 Wait for a few minutes and observe the beads. The bead in the metal spoon will slide faster than the ones in the wooden and plastic spoons.

The STEM behind it

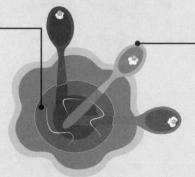

Metals are good conductors of heat, whereas plastic and wood are bad conductors of heat. Thus, the metal spoon becomes hotter more quickly than the other two spoons. The butter begins to melt making the bead slide down the spoon.

When we place the spoons in boiling water, heat is transferred from the water molecules to the molecules of the spoons.

22
HOT ICE

Life Connect: Heating pads and hand warmers

1

Take a flask and put 160 g of sodium acetate in it. Now, slowly add 30 ml of water to it.

2

With the help of an adult, heat the flask until the crystals dissolve in water. Stir continuously while heating the solution.

3

Remove the flask from the hot plate and cover it. Now, place it in the refrigerator to chill.

4

Next, place two to three sodium acetate crystals at the center of a plate. Now, pour the sodium acetate solution very slowly on top of the crystals.

5

The crystals will grow just as you pour the solution to form amazing towers!

The STEM behind it

The cold sodium acetate solution is an example of a supercool liquid, i.e., it exists as a liquid below its usual melting point.

The crystals on the plate act as a nesting site for other crystals to grow in the solution.

The crystallization process releases a lot of heat so the crystal 'towers' are hot to touch and hence are called hot ice.

23
STEAM VOLCANO

DIFFICULTY LEVEL
Adult supervision required

Life Connect: Acid-base reaction

You Need
- White vinegar
- Baking soda
- Measuring cups
- Film canister
- Clay
- Food coloring
- A tray

1 Measure equal amounts of baking soda and white vinegar and pour them into separate cups.

2 Add a few drops of red food color to the cup of vinegar. Doing so will add a visual effect to the 'lava' that will erupt during the experiment.

4 Remove the lid of the film canister and push it into the tip of the volcano. The open side of the film should face up.

3 Using modeling clay, build the structure of a volcano as shown in the picture. Make it as tall as you can.

5 Pour baking soda into the film canister you had placed in the volcano.

6

Very carefully, pour the colored vinegar into the film canister and stand back.

7

The volcano erupts!

The STEM behind it

An acid-base reaction takes place between vinegar and baking soda. When combined they form carbon dioxide.

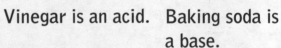

Vinegar is an acid.

Baking soda is a base.

The carbon dioxide rises and creates the 'eruption' or 'explosion' effect in the volcano.

24
ELEPHANT TOOTHPASTE

Life Connect: Decomposition reaction; Role of catalyst in chemical reactions

You Need
- Warm water
- Yeast
- 3% or 6% hydrogen peroxide
- Food coloring
- An empty plastic bottle
- Dish soap
- Funnel

1 Mix two tbsp of warm water and one tbsp of yeast in a bowl until the yeast completely dissolves in water.

2 Take an empty bottle. Using a funnel pour ½ cup of hydrogen peroxide into it.

3 Add a few drops of red food coloring into the bottle. This is just to add visual effect to the experiment.

4 Add a big squirt of dish soap into the bottle and swirl it gently.

5 At last, pour the mixture of water and yeast into the bottle. Step back and watch carefully what happens next.

6 A foamy toothpaste-like substance comes out of the bottle—but it is so big that it almost looks fit for an elephant!

The STEM behind it

When hydrogen peroxide comes into contact with the yeast, it starts breaking down into water and oxygen.

Being a gas, oxygen tries to escape the liquid. The dish soap traps the oxygen bubbles, forming a foam like substance popularly known as the elephant toothpaste.

Hydrogen peroxide is an unstable compound which slowly decomposes into water and oxygen under normal conditions.

Yeast acts as a catalyst in this experiment.

25
HOW WATER ABSORBS HEAT

Life Connect: Effects of rising temperatures on the ocean

DIFFICULTY LEVEL

Adult supervision required

You Need
- Two balloons
- Water
- A candle
- Lighter

1  Inflate a balloon to a normal size. Put some water into the second balloon and inflate it such that it is a little smaller than the first balloon.

2  Light the candle using a lighter.

3 Hold the balloon filled with air over the candle as shown in the picture.

4 It will pop quickly as it is exposed to heat from the candle flame.

5  Now, hold the water-filled balloon over the candle. It shouldn't pop!

The STEM behind it

Air has a lower specific heat capacity than water. This means the amount of heat required to warm up air is lesser than that required to heat water.

The air inside the first balloon absorbs heat very quickly and expands. Hence, the balloon pops!

The water in the second balloon absorbs a lot of heat before it begins to get hot so the second balloon doesn't pop.

26
LET US BUILD A THERMOMETER

Life Connect: Measuring temperature

You Need
- Water
- Rubbing alcohol
- Food coloring
- A marker
- A plastic bottle
- A pair of scissors
- Card
- A clear straw
- Modeling clay
- Ice cubes
- A shallow container

1

Fill half of a bottle with an equal amount of rubbing alcohol and water. Add a few drops of food colouring to it.

2

Put a straw in the bottle such that it is submerged in water, but remains just above the bottom of the bottle.

3

Wrap modeling clay around the straw at the mouth of the bottle and seal it. Make sure it is airtight.

4

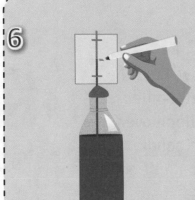

Blow gently into the straw. You will see that water rises up in the straw.

5

With the help of an adult, cut two slits on a piece of card.

6

Slide the card over the straw. Blow into the straw. Now, mark the level of water , where it stopped, on the card using a marker.

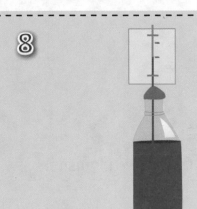

7 Keep the thermometer in a container filled with warm water. Watch the level of water rise in the straw. Once the water stops rising, mark the new level of water.

8 Take out the thermometer from the warm water and let the level of water settle.

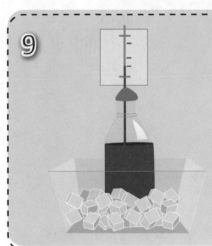

9 Now, place the thermometer in a container with ice cubes in it. Watch the level of water inside the straw drop.

The STEM behind it

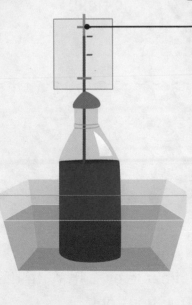

Air inside the bottle expands due to the heat from the water in the container. Due to this, the water is pushed up and its level in the straw rises.

When the bottle is placed in the container with ice cubes, the air inside the bottle contracts. Hence, the water goes down and its level in the straw falls.

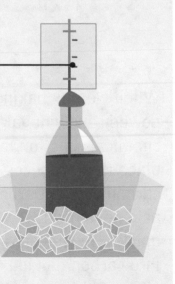

43

27
INVISIBLE FIRE EXTINGUISHER

Life Connect: CO_2 fire extinguishers

DIFFICULTY LEVEL

Adult supervision required

You Need
- A candle
- A plastic bottle
- Baking soda
- White vinegar
- A match box
- A funnel

1 Fill a bottle 1/4th with white vinegar.

2 Place a funnel at the mouth of the bottle and add 3 tbsp of baking soda into it.

3 You'll see a lot of bubble forming in the bottle.

4 Let the reaction calm down and the bubbles settle. In the meantime, light a candle and keep it aside.

5  Slowly pour the liquid over the flame. The candle flame goes out in no time!

The STEM behind it

When we mix baking powder and vinegar, a chemical reaction takes place that produces carbonic acid. Carbonic acid being unstable quickly decomposes into carbon dioxide (CO_2) and water.

Carbon dioxide pushes air out of the bottle and takes up all the space inside it.

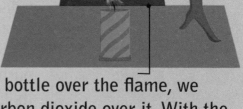

When we tilt the bottle over the flame, we actually 'pour' carbon dioxide over it. With the lack of oxygen, the flame goes out!

28

SECRET MESSAGE

Life Connect: Oxidation

DIFFICULTY LEVEL

1

Cut a lemon into half and squeeze the juice into a small bowl. The lemon juice will act as your ink.

2

Dip a cotton bud in lemon juice and write your message on a piece of plain paper.

3

You will observe that the message is visible as long as the paper is wet. Once the paper dries completely, your message disappears.

4

With the help of an adult, hold this paper over a heat source, such as a lighted candle or an incandescent bulb.

5

After sometime, your secret message slowly becomes visible!

The STEM behind it

Lemon juice contains carbon-based compounds that are colorless at room temperature. When we write the message, these carbon-based compounds are absorbed by the paper.

On heating the paper, carbon is released from the lemon juice. It comes in contact with air and oxidizes.

This turns your secret message (written with lemon juice) brown, making it visible.

COLORFUL CONVECTION CURRENTS

Life Connect: Land and sea breeze

You Need
- Four identical glass or plastic bottles
- Hot and cold water
- Yellow and blue food coloring
- 3x5-inch index cards

1

Fill two bottles with cold water and two bottles with hot water to the brim. You may mark the bottles HOT and COLD using a marker and masking tape.

2

Cold   Hot

Pour a few drops of blue food colouring into the bottles of cold water and yellow food colouring into the bottles of hot water.

3

Hot

cold

With the help of an adult, place an index card over the mouth of one of the bottles containing hot water. Holding the card, carefully turn the bottle upside down and rest it on the bottle of cold water such that the bottles are positioned mouth to mouth with the card in between.

4

Hot

cold

Holding the top bottle, carefully remove the card from between the two bottles. Observe what happens to the water in both the bottles.

5

Repeat the third and fourth step with the bottle of cold water on top of the hot water bottle. What happens to the water in the bottles this time?

The STEM behind it

This movement of warm and cold waters in the bottles occurs due to convection—a form of heat transfer by movement in gas or liquid.
Convection may also be caused due to differences in density of gases or liquids.

When you place the bottle of cold water on top, the hot water being less dense rises into the bottle of cold water (i.e., the top bottle).

This can be observed when the yellow and blue food colouring mixes and the water turns green.

30
TEA BAG ROCKET

Life Connect: Density difference and convection currents

You Need
- A tea bag
- A pair of scissors
- A shallow plate
- A candle
- Lighter

1

Cut the top of the tea bag using scissors.

2

Remove the string/staples if any and empty out the tea leaves into a separate bowl.

3
Unfold the tea bag and straighten it. Then, roll it such that it looks like a hollow cylinder.

4

Keep the tea bag upright on a plate. With the help of an adult, light the top rim of the tea bag around its edges.

5

Stand back and let the bag burn completely.

6

The tea bag lifts off the plate and quickly rises into the air. It then descends slowly as it cools.

The STEM behind it

When the tea bag is burnt, it warms the air inside and above it. This gives rise to a thermal or convection current.

The density of air inside the tea bag cylinder is less than that the outside.

The light warm air inside the bag rises and the denser cool air outside the cylinder moves in from the bottom of the cylinder to take its place.

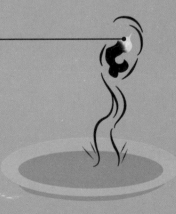

When the bag burns, it changes into ash and smoke. It is so light in weight that the hot air quickly lifts it upwards!

SODA GEYSER

Life Connect: Carbonation and nucleation

You Need
- One piece of 8x10 inch construction paper
- Tape
- 1 bottle of Diet soda or Coke
- Two rolls of Mentos mints

1 Set the bottle of Diet Coke on a flat surface. Remove its lid.

2 Roll construction paper into a tube and secure it with a tape. Make sure the tube is just big enough to hold the loose Mentos.

3 Put seven Mentos mints into the tube.

4 Now, hold your finger at the bottom of the tube and position it directly over the mouth of the bottle.

5 Now, remove your finger and drop all the mints into the bottle immediately.

6 Stand back and watch the amazing soda pop geyser!

The STEM behind it

Diet Coke is a carbonated beverage (which means it contains dissolved carbon dioxide (CO_2)).

The Mentos' surface is rough and has many tiny pits.

Mentos mints being heavy, drop to the bottom of the Diet Coke bottle.

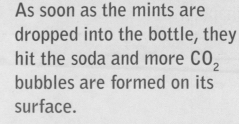

As soon as the mints are dropped into the bottle, they hit the soda and more CO_2 bubbles are formed on its surface.

These bubbles quickly rise to the surface of the Diet Coke and result in an incredible soda eruption!

THERMAL-POWERED FLOWER

Life Connect: Wind turbines

DIFFICULTY LEVEL 🔴🔴⚪⚪⚪

You Need
- Modeling clay
- Straws
- Skewers
- Colored paper
- Scissors
- A candle
- A pencil
- Tape
- A ruler
- A lighter
- An eye screw

1

Using scissors, trim the straw and the skewer such that the skewer is an inch longer than the straw. Keep it aside.

2

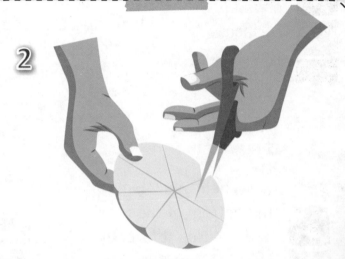

Draw a flower and a leaf on colored papers and cut them along the edges as shown.

3

Twist the petals such that they create a fan shape.

4

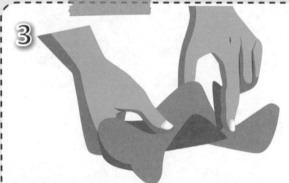

Keep the straw upright and wrap the clay around it at the bottom.

5

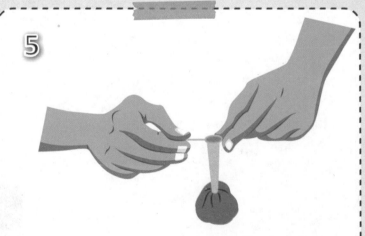

Secure the eye screw on the straw using tape and tape the cut-out of the leaf on the eye screw.

6

Attach the flat end of the skewer to the bottom of the flower using some modeling clay. Carefully place the skewer inside the straw so that its other end rests on the table.

7

Light four candles and place them at the base of the straw as shown.

8

The flower will start spinning in sometime!

The STEM behind it

The flames of the candle heat up the air around them, causing the air to expand and become lighter than the surrounding cooler air.

The heated air rises upwards, creating a gentle, warm breeze. This causes the flower to rotate!

EXPERIMENTS WITH

LIGHT

Light is a form of energy. There are different sources of light. Sunlight is the natural source of light on Earth. The other sources of light include electric bulbs and LEDs. We can see things around us either because they give off light or reflect light that falls on them.

Light can travel in all mediums and even in vacuum. It usually travels in a straight line. However, when light passes from one medium to another, it bends or turns. This phenomenon is called refraction of light. When light falls on an opaque object, it bounces back or reflects. This phenomenon is called reflection.

LIGHT WRITER

Life Connect: Light-emitting diodes

You Need
- An LED light of any color of your choice
- Digital camera with adjustable time or shutter speed
- Sticky tape
- A button battery

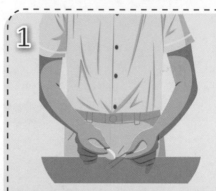

1

Connect the LED light to the battery by putting one of the prongs on either side. The longer prong of the LED should be connected to the positive pole of the battery.
The LED should light up.

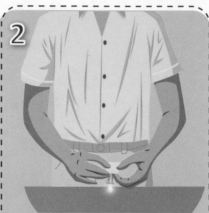

2

Using sticky tape, fasten the prongs of the lighted LED firmly to the battery so that it doesn't wobble. Your pen is ready!

3

Next, ask an adult to set the camera on a stand. The camera should be set to a long exposure time or slow shutter-closing speed. Dim the lights and darken the room as much as you can.

4

Pointing the LED towards the camera, write something in the air from right to left. For example, Hello. The word will appear on the camera screen!

The STEM behind it

The right camera setting makes writing with the LED successful.
The shutter of the camera allows light into it and makes pictures. This happens for a fraction of a second.

When the camera is set to a long exposure mode or a slow shutter-closing speed, the shutter remains open for a longer time than usual. This lets the camera capture light continuously while we are writing using the LED. Thus, our message is captured!

WORM CHANGING DIRECTION

DIFFICULTY LEVEL

Life Connect: Refraction of light

1
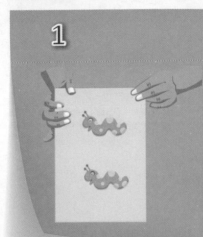
Draw two worms on a sheet of white paper. One worm at the top and another at the bottom of the sheet. Make these worms point towards the same direction.

3
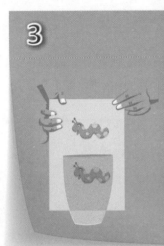
Next, slowly lower the piece of paper behind it. Is there any change in the drawing? Certainly not!

2
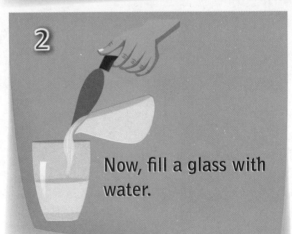
Now, fill a glass with water.

4

Look through the glass again. The worm at the bottom of the paper has changed direction!

The STEM behind it

It's an optical illusion due to refraction of light!

Light first travels through the glass into the water and bends once.
It then travels out of the glass and into the air and bends again.

This results in the crossing of paths of light. Thus, the worm appears to be flipped horizontally.

LET'S MAKE A FLASHLIGHT

Life Connect: Working of a light bulb

DIFFICULTY LEVEL
■ ■ □ □ □
Adult supervision required

You Need
- An empty plastic bottle
- Aluminum foil
- Cotton
- Tape
- Wire cut into three pieces with bare ends
- Paper clips
- A pencil
- Two 1.5 V batteries
- Paper fasteners
- Scissors
- A small bulb in a holder

1
Remove the cap of the bottle. With the help of an adult, cut off its top using scissors. Using a sharp object, such as a pencil, make two holes on the side of the bottle.

2
Cover the inside of the bottle top with foil such that the shiny side faces outwards. Secure the foil with tape.

3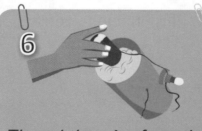
Take two pieces of wire and attach them firmly to the bulb-holder. Take help from an adult if required.

4
Now, take the batteries and tape them together such that the top of one battery touches the base of the other. Then, fix the third piece of wire to the lower battery using tape.

5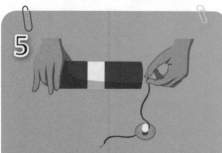
Using tape, secure one of the wires from the bulb holder to the terminal of the top battery.

6
Thread the wire from the bottom battery through the lower hole in the bottle. Put cotton into the bottle and insert the batteries.

7
Now, thread the wire from the bulb holder through the top hole in the bottle. Attach both wires to paper fasteners and push them in.

8

Place the bulb holder on the batteries inside the bottle. Then, secure the center of the bottle top over the bulb using tape.

9

Fix a paper clip under the lower paper fastener. This will act as a switch for the flashlight.

10

Fix the other end of the paper clip on the top paper fastener. The flashlight gets turned on and it lights up.

The STEM behind it

The paper clip acts as a switch for the flashlight. When we fix the other end of the paper clip to the top fastener, the switch is pushed into the ON position. It makes contact with the wires connected to the batteries. A flow of electricity begins which activates the bulb in the holder and it starts to glows.

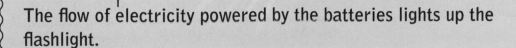

The flow of electricity powered by the batteries lights up the flashlight.

36

MAKE A CAMERA OBSCURA

Life Connect: Image formation in real life

DIFFICULTY LEVEL

Adult supervision required

You Need
- Paper towel roll
- Tracing paper
- Aluminum foil
- Clear tape and dark tape
- Decorative sheet Wax paper
- Scissors or craft knife
- A board pin

1

Cut off two inches from a paper towel roll using a craft knife or scissors as shown.

2

Cover one end of the roll with tracing paper. Secure its ends on the roll using tape.

3

Now, reattach the piece of the roll that was cut off, to the end of the roll with wax paper.

4

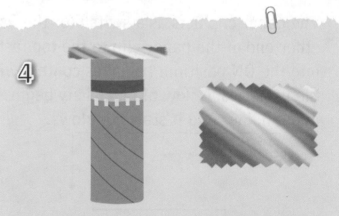

Wrap aluminum foil around the end of the roll closest to the wax paper section and secure it carefully using tape. Make sure that the shinier side of the foil faces down.

5

Poke a small hole in the center of the foil using a board pin.

6

Next, cover the roll with decorative paper. Your camera obscura is ready.

7 Go out and look at a tree through the camera obscura. Keep the side with the tiny hole away from yourself. You will see an upside-down image of the tree, inside the camera.

The STEM behind it

A camera obscura works on the rectilinear theory of light, which means that light travels in a straight line.

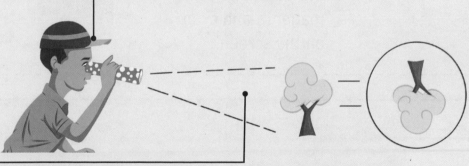

A ray of light from the top of the tree falls at a point on the tracing paper after passing through the tiny hole. A ray from the bottom of the tree falls at another point on the paper. Similarly, rays from the tree fall at different points on the tracing paper after passing through the hole. These points of light together make up an image of the tree, which is upside down, inside the camera. Any object that you will look at in this manner will appear upside down.

37

COLORFUL SHADOWS

Life Connect: Light receptors

You Need
- Red, blue and green light bulbs
- An electrical extension board
- A white surface or screen, such as a wall or poster board
- A pencil

1

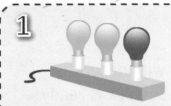

Set up the bulbs on an electrical extension board such that the green bulb is in between the red and the blue bulb.

2

Place the holder with the bulbs in front of a white screen such that light from all the three bulbs falls on the same area of the screen. Darken the room as much as you can. Then, turn on the light bulbs. Adjust the place of the bulbs until the light on the screen is almost or totally white.

3

Place a pencil close to the screen. You will observe three shadows of the pencil: yellow, magenta and cyan on the screen.

4

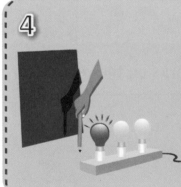

Now, turn off the green and blue light bulbs. Place the pencil close to the screen again. This time you will see a dark shadow.

5

Turn off only the green light bulb this time. When the red and blue light bulbs shine, light gets scattered off the screen and we see a magenta color on the screen.

6

Place the pencil close to the screen again. This time you can see a red and a blue shadow of the pencil on the screen.

7

Repeat steps 5 and 6 with another light bulb turned off while the other two remain on and observe what happens.

The STEM behind it

When all the three light bulbs shine together, the screen looks white because these three colored lights stimulate all three types of cones in your eyes almost equally, blending the signals they send and we see white. We can see shadows of different colors by blocking different combinations of light.

If we turn off the green light, leaving only the blue and red lights on, the screen will appear magenta.

When we hold a pencil in front of the screen, the pencil blocks the light coming from the red bulb in one place, leaving a blue shadow; in the other location it blocks the light from the blue bulb, leaving a red shadow.

38

LET'S MAKE A KALEIDOSCOPE

Life Connect: Reflection of light

DIFFICULTY LEVEL

Adult supervision required

You Need
- Clear plastic report cover
- A paper towel roll
- A pencil
- Scissors
- Transparent tape
- Plastic wrap
- Transparent objects like beads and sequins
- Wax paper
- Wrapping paper
- Black construction paper
- Sticky tape

1

Cut an 8x4-inch rectangle using a clear plastic report cover.

2

Draw three horizontal lines across the rectangle and split it into four parts such that the first three parts are around 1.25-inch wide and the last part is 1/4th wide.

3

Fold the plastic cover along the lines to form a triangular shape such that the 1/4th inch wide strip remains on the outside and acts as a flap.

4

Using transparent tape, secure the strip along the edge of the triangle.

5

Cut a paper towel roll into the same size as the triangle plastic cover (around 8-inch). Now, slide the plastic triangle into the paper towel roll.

6

Next, trace a circle on black construction paper. The circle should be slightly bigger than the diameter of the roll. Then, poke a hole through the center of the circle. Make sure the circle is large enough for you to see through it.

7

Turn the paper towel roll and tape the circle over one of its ends.

8

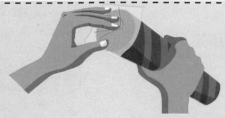

Cut a 4-inch square from the plastic wrap. Place it over the other end of the paper towel roll. Poke the piece of wrap down into the plastic triangle with your fingers such that it forms a little pouch.

9

Fill the pouch with beads and sequins. Then, place a 4-inch square piece of waxed paper over the pouch and around the end of the paper towel roll. Secure it using sticky tape.

10

Next decorate your kaleidoscope using wrapping paper. Hold up the kaleidoscope to one eye, facing the light, and look through it. You will see a beautiful pattern inside the kaleidoscope. Rotate or tilt the tube again to see more symmetrical images.

The STEM behind it

We can see patterns inside a kaleidoscope due to the reflection of light. Light travels in a straight line. When light falls on a shiny surface, it bounces back in the direction it came from. This is called reflection.

When we point the kaleidoscope towards light, light enters the kaleidoscope. Then, it is reflected by the shiny objects—beads and sequins inside the kaleidoscope to create magnificent picturesque patterns.

39

MAGIC COIN

Life Connect: Illusions due to refraction of light

DIFFICULTY LEVEL

You Need
- A coin
- Water
- A clear drinking glass
- A saucer

1

Place a coin on a flat surface, such as a desk or a table.

2

Place the bottom of a clear drinking glass over the coin.

3

Cover the mouth of the glass with a saucer. Observe the coin through the side of the glass. You can still see the coin in it.

4

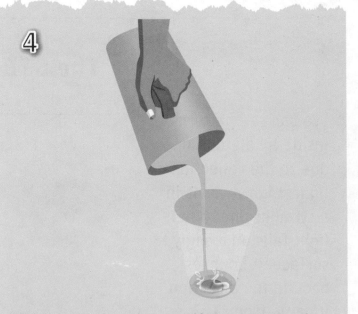

Now, take the saucer off the mouth of the glass and pour water into it.

5

Once the glass is full, cover it with the saucer. Look through the side of the glass again. Can you still see the coin?

6

Remove the saucer from the glass and look inside the glass from the top. The magic coin is right there!

The STEM behind it

The coin seems to disappear because of the refraction of light. Light rays travel through the glass and reach our eyes when the glass is empty. Therefore, we can see the coin.

When the glass is filled with water, the light rays travel through water, get refracted and cannot reach our eyes. The image of the coin is formed near the top of the glass due to the refraction of light. Since the top of the glass is covered with the saucer, it seems that the coin has disappeared.

EXPERIMENTS WITH

SOUND

Sound is a form of energy. It is produced when objects vibrate, i.e., shaken back and forth. These vibrations travel through different mediums in the form of waves. When sound waves reach our ears, they make the eardrums vibrate too, hence, we hear sound.

Sound cannot travel in vacuum. It needs a medium such as air, water or a solid object to travel through. The loudness of the sound is determined by its waves. Bigger the waves, louder is the sound.

The pitch of the sound is determined by vibrations. When objects vibrate fast, they create a high-pitched sound. When objects vibrate slowly, low-pitched sounds are produced.

SINGING TUBES

Life Connect: Sound Waves

DIFFICULTY LEVEL

Adult supervision required

You Need
- A piece of heavy wire mesh
- A long, hollow metal tube
- Propane torch
- A stick

1

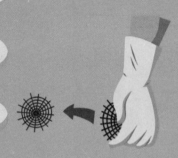

Carefully, fold the piece of heavy wire mesh into a bowl shape. Make it such that it fits into the metal tube. For this, it needs to have a diameter slightly larger than the inside diameter of the metal tube.

2

Using a stick, insert the mesh into one end of the tube. It should be about 4-inch from the end of the tube.

3

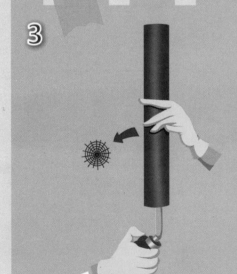

Light the propane torch. With the help of an adult, position the metal tube over the propane torch to directly heat the wire mesh inside the tube. Heat it for approximately 10-20 seconds.

4 Remove the tube from the propane torch and hold it vertically for some time. A loud sound will begin to echo from the tube.

The STEM behind it

The wire mesh placed inside the tube is made of metal. When it is heated, the metal will retain the heat for quite some time. This heated mesh heats the surrounding air, which then rises through the tube.

As the hot air rises, cooler air from the room flows into the tube through the wire mesh. This makes the air turbulent, setting up vibrations inside the tube. Therefore, the tube begins to 'sing'.

41
BUILD A DISK SIREN

Life Connect: Understanding how sirens work

You Need
- A protractor
- Scissors or a paper knife
- A geometric compass
- A pencil
- A piece of thick construction paper
- Paper clip
- Paper towel
- Round-hole puncher
- A double-sided foam tape
- A small safety or baby fan with soft foam blades and battery
- A straw

1

Draw an 8 cm circle using a compass on a construction paper. Draw two smaller circles with 6 and 7 cm radius within the same circle.

2

With the help of an adult, cut along the outermost circle using scissors or a paper knife.

3

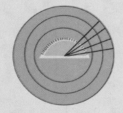

Now, draw lines at 15° intervals through the center of the circle using a protractor.

4

Using a hole puncher, punch holes at every intersection of lines on the 7 cm circle.

5

Next, punch holes at every second intersection of lines on the 6 cm circle.

6

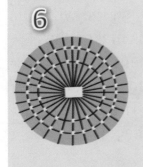

Cut a small piece of foam tape and stick it at the center of one side of the circle. Your circular disk is ready.

7

Make a small hole through the center of the circle and foam tape.

8 With the help of an adult, mount the circular disk to the fan blades. You may remove the blades, attach the disk to the fan and remount the blades once the disk gets attached.

9 Ask an adult to turn on the fan. Aim a straw at the outer ring of the holes and blow through it. Can you listen to the pitch of the sound produced?

10 Now, move the straw to the inner rings of holes and blow through it. Is there a change in the pitch of the sound?

The STEM behind it

When we blow air through the straw on the rings of the disk, the flow of air is alternatively interrupted and allowed to pass as the disk spins. This fluctuation in air pressure produces a series of pressure waves that we perceive as sound. The number of holes on the disk and its rotation speed impacts the sound produced. The more the number of holes on the disk and higher its speed, the higher the pitch of sound.

FEELING SOUND

DIFFICULTY LEVEL

You Need
- A balloon
- A speaker

Life Connect: Distance and sound

1 Blow up a balloon. Tie its end when it is almost filled with air.

2 Hold the balloon in front of your face with both hands and say something at a medium volume. You should feel the balloon vibrate. Now, try raising and lowering your voice. Is there any change in the vibrations on the balloon?

3 Now, play a song on your speaker. Hold the balloon near the speaker. Observe the intensity of the vibrations on the balloon. Increase or decrease the volume of the speaker. You will notice that the intensity of the vibrations on the balloon changes too.

4 Next, place the balloon a little away from the speaker. Place your hand on the balloon. Do you still feel vibrations on the balloon?

5

At last, place the balloon far from the speaker. Are the vibrations the same as observed when the balloon was near the speaker?

The STEM behind it

When we hold the balloon near the speaker, sound hits the balloon and it vibrates.

When we hold the balloon far from the speaker, sound from the speaker causes the air around it to vibrate. The vibrations spread through the air, hit the balloon and it vibrates.

When we increase the distance between the speaker and the balloon, sound waves spread over a greater area, hence the intensity of the vibrations decrease. Thus, we feel little to no vibrations on the balloon.

43

DIY PHONE SPEAKERS

Life Connect: How the shape of a medium can amplify the sound

You Need
- Two medium-sized plastic cups
- One kraft tube
- A mobile phone or any other device to play music
- A knife
- A marker
- Acrylic paint or wrapping paper
- Hot glue

1

Measure the width and depth of the mobile phone you shall use for the experiment. Cut a slot in the kraft tube with the same dimensions.

2

Decorate your kraft tube and plastic cups in beautiful designs with acrylic paints or wrapping paper.

3

Now, hold the kraft tube to one side of the plastic cup near the bottom. Trace the edge of the tube on the cup. With the help of an adult, cut out the hole with a paper knife. Do this for the second cup as well.

4

Carefully insert the kraft tube into the holes of the cups as shown. Use hot glue to secure the tube in place.

5

At last, place the mobile phone into the slot on the kraft tube. Play some tunes. You will notice that the music from the cups is louder than the music from the mobile phone.

The STEM behind it

Sound that is directed into a smaller angle, sounds louder.

When we place the mobile phone into the slot of the kraft tube and play some tunes on it, sound travels into the plastic cups. The conical shape of the cups direct the sound from a narrow area to a wider area. It allows less sound to scatter in different directions, thus amplifying it more than the phone's speaker.

44
LET'S SEE SOUND

Real life application: How we hear sound?

DIFFICULTY LEVEL

You Need
- A glass bowl
- Plastic wrap
- Handful of uncooked rice
- A large rubber band
- A portable bluetooth speaker
- A phone or device to connect to the speaker

1 Switch on the bluetooth speaker and connect it to your phone. Then, place the speaker in a glass bowl.

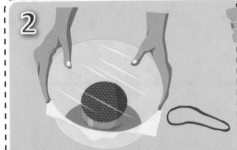

2 Cover the top of the bowl with plastic wrap. Make sure the wrap tightly covers the mouth. You may also secure it by wrapping a rubber band around the edges of the bowl.

3 Put a handful of uncooked rice over the plastic wrap.

4 Now, play some music on your phone or device on a low volume. Gradually increase the volume. You will see the rice granules moving around on the plastic wrap. You may continue to increase the volume and observe the changes to the rice every time.

The STEM behind it

Sound is a wave that is produced by back and forth vibrations of particles in the air or any other medium.

When we play music on the speaker, sound waves travel from the speaker to the plastic wrap, causing it to vibrate. Increasing the volume adds energy to the sound waves, resulting in more vibrations. These vibrations are big enough to move the uncooked rice grains on the plastic wrap.

EXPERIMENTS WITH

ELECTRICITY

Electricity is the flow of negatively charged particles (i.e. electrons) from one place to another. It is of two kinds—current electricity and static electricity. From lighting homes to communication, electricity is used in different ways in our daily lives.

Electricity is generated from different sources such as coal, water, solar energy and natural gas. It is produced at power plants where a fuel is burnt to boil water. The steam produced is then used to spin turbines. The spinning turbines turn generators to make electricity.

45
MAKE A SIMPLE SWITCH

Life Connect: Electric switches

DIFFICULTY LEVEL

1

Take the piece of cardboard and lay the paperclip on it. Push a thumbtack through one end of the paperclip securing it to the cardboard.

2

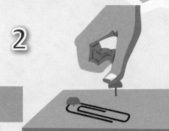

Push the other thumbtack into the cardboard such that the paperclip can be rotated to touch both the thumbtacks. This is your switch.

3

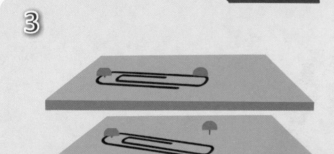

Rotate the paperclip such that it touches the other thumbtack. The switch is now closed. Next, move the paperclip away from the thumbtack, the switch is now open.

4

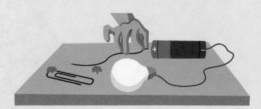

Now, connect a piece of wire from one end of a battery to a bulb. Secure it using tape. Similarly, connect another piece of wire to the other end of the battery.

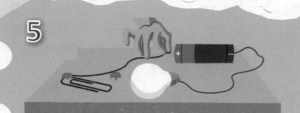

5

Next, connect the other end of the wire on the battery to one side of the switch by wrapping it around the thumbtack.

6

Connect the last wire between the switch and the bulb. Close the switch by touching the paperclip to the other thumbtack. The bulb lights up!

The STEM behind it

To power a light bulb, we need a circuit-an unbroken path for electricity to flow.

The wires, battery, bulb, and switch together make an electric circuit. A switch is simply a break in the circuit.

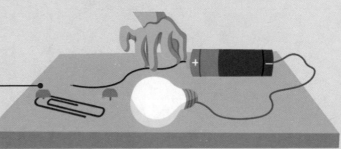

When the paperclip touches both the thumbtacks, the switch is closed (indicating that the circuit is complete) and the flow of electricity begins, lighting up the bulb. When the paperclip is moved away from the other thumbtack, the switch opens (indicating that the circuit is broken) and interrupts the flow of electricity and the light bulb switches off.

46

DANCING HEART

Life Connect: Lorentz Force

DIFFICULTY LEVEL

Adult supervision required

You Need
- A spool of copper wire
- AA battery
- Pliers or wire cutter
- 0.5x0.125-inch Neodymium disc magnets

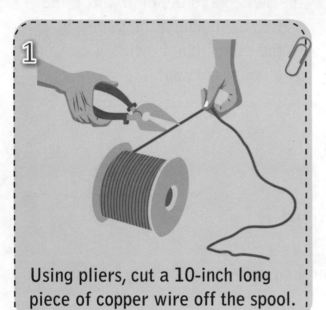

1 Using pliers, cut a 10-inch long piece of copper wire off the spool.

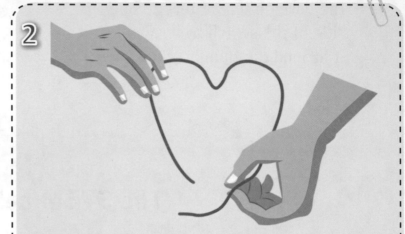

2 Mold it into the shape of a heart. Try to make it as symmetrical as possible.

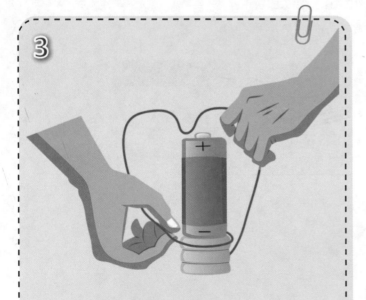

3 Wrap the open end of the heart around an AA battery once or twice. This is to create the base of the heart that will wrap the magnets.

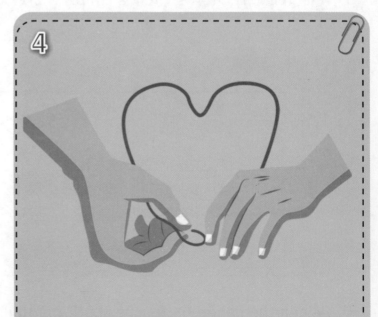

4 Now, carefully remove the wire wrap from the battery and widen it slightly with your fingers.

5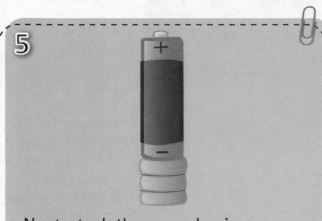

Next, stack three neodymium magnets one upon the other. Place the AA battery on the stack of magnets. Its negative side should be facing the magnets.

6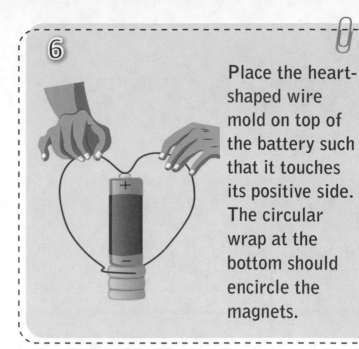

Place the heart-shaped wire mold on top of the battery such that it touches its positive side. The circular wrap at the bottom should encircle the magnets.

7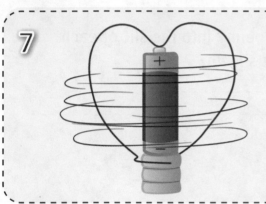

You will notice that the heart-shaped wire starts to spin!

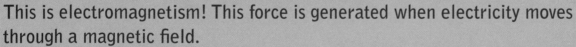

The STEM behind it

This is electromagnetism! This force is generated when electricity moves through a magnetic field.

The copper wire conducts electricity from one end of the battery to another.

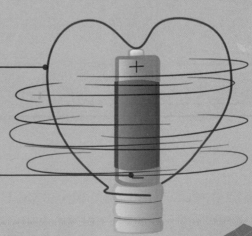

When electricity moves through the magnets on the negative side of the battery, an electromagnetic force is created, which causes the heart-shaped wire to spin.

47
LEMON BATTERY

Life Connect: Voltaic cell

You Need
- Three big lemons
- Three pennies
- Three zinc-galvanized nails
- Four to five sets of alligator clips
- A mini LED bulb
- A knife

Using a knife, cut a penny-sized slit in all three lemons.

2

Insert a penny into the slit of each lemon as shown.

3 Mark a point on one of the lemons opposite the penny. Push a zinc-galvanized nail at this point. Make sure that the nail and the penny are placed securely on the lemon. Repeat this for the other two lemons.

4

Connect a nail on one lemon to a penny on another lemon using a set of alligator clips.

5

Similarly, connect all three lemons together. Make sure that each set of alligator clips connects a nail to a penny.

6

Now, you shall have one open penny and one open nail. Connect one of the alligator clips to the open penny. Next, connect the last alligator clip to the only open nail. You must be left with two unused clips on two separate alligator clips.

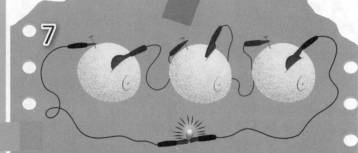

7

Attach the two loose clips to the LED bulb. The bulb is powered by electrical energy and starts glowing!

The STEM behind it

The lemon battery is an example of voltaic battery. They require three things: two different metals that act as electrodes and an acidic solution (electrolyte) that conducts electricity.

The metal electrodes used here are zinc (nail) and copper (penny). The citric acid acts as the electrolyte.

Setting up the alligator clips completes the circuit. The electrons flow out of the penny (copper) and into the nail (zinc) through the acid inside the lemon, lighting up the LED bulb.

48

GHOSTS BOOGIE

DIFFICULTY LEVEL

Life Connect: Static electricity

You Need
- A piece of cardboard
- Green and black construction paper
- White tissue paper
- A black marker
- Glue
- Scissors
- A balloon
- A woolen cloth

1

Use black construction paper to draw a dry spooky tree, a tall rectangle and tombstones, and cut these out. Then, draw and cut out some pieces of grass from green construction paper.

2

Glue the rectangular piece onto the back of the tree.

4

Draw and cut out ghosts using white tissue paper. Using a marker, draw their faces.

3

Now, glue the tree, tombstones and pieces of grass onto the cardboard. Glue the ghosts to the back of the tombstones on the cardboard.

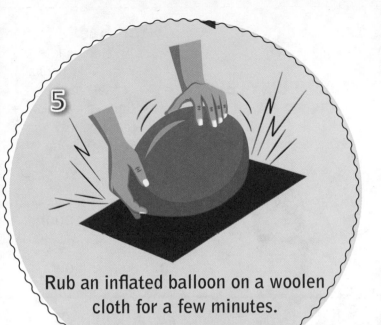

5 Rub an inflated balloon on a woolen cloth for a few minutes.

6 Now, hold the balloon above the cardboard and hover it over the tombstones. The ghosts will rise and dance!

The STEM behind it

It's because of static electricity!

When we rub the balloon on the woolen cloth, electrons from the cloth move onto the balloon. The balloon now has more electrons and thus acquires an overall negative charge, generating static electricity.

When we position the balloon over the ghosts, the negatively charged balloon attracts the positively charged ghosts. The ghosts being light, rise and dance as a result of static electricity!

SEPARATE SALT AND PEPPER

Life Connect: Static electricity

DIFFICULTY LEVEL

You Need
- An empty plate
- Two tablespoons of table salt
- One teaspoon of black pepper
- A plastic comb

1  Add two tablespoons of salt into an empty plate.

2  Add one teaspoon of black pepper to the salt. Now, gently shake the plate to mix the two.

3  Take a plastic comb and rub it through your hair a few times.

The STEM behind it

The comb had a neutral charge before it was rubbed through your hair.

Rubbing the comb gave it an electric charge. This happened because electrons from your hair moved onto the comb. The comb gained more electrons than it already had, thus making it negatively charged.

4  Now, position the comb over the salt and pepper on the plate. Did the pepper jump onto the comb?

 Since, pepper is positively charged and is lighter than salt, it jumps to the comb.

HUMAN CONDUCTOR OF ELECTRICITY

DIFFICULTY LEVEL

⬭ ⬭ ⬬ ⬬ ⬬

Adult supervision required

Life Connect: Conductors and insulators

You Need
- An inflated balloon
- A sweater
- Fluorescent light

1

Blow a balloon and rub it vigorously on a woolen sweater for some time.

2

Now, bring the balloon close to the bulb. What happens? You will notice a flicker of light in the bulb!

3

Next, move the balloon up and down, keeping it at the same distance from the bulb. Observe that the flicker of light follows the movement of the balloon.

4

Now, gently touch the balloon to the bulb. Did you see a spark? Is it possible?

The STEM behind it

When we rub the balloon on the woolen sweater, the balloon becomes negatively charged. Electrons from the sweater move to the balloon and stay there.

The inside of the fluorescent bulb has phosphors and mercury vapor.
When the negatively charged balloon is brought close to the bulb, the electrons collide with the mercury vapor and emit ultraviolet light. This causes the phosphors inside the bulb to glow.

GRAPHITE CIRCUIT

Life Connect: Conductors of electricity

DIFFICULTY LEVEL
● ● ○ ○ ○

You Need
- A sheet of paper
- A graphite pencil (art pencil)
- Foil
- Tape
- 9V battery
- LEDs

1

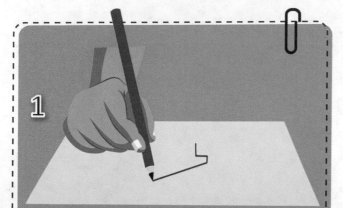

Draw a simple picture on a piece of paper using a graphite pencil. Make sure the lines of your drawing are thick and are connected to each other. For example, draw a house.

2

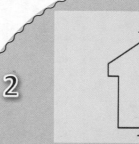

Leave around 1 cm gap on the opposite sides of the house, as shown. Mark positive and negative lines on these ends.

3

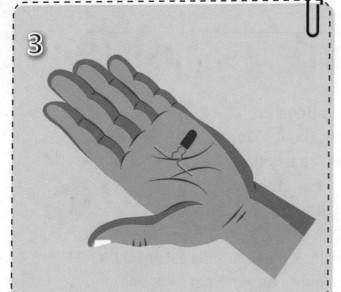

Take an LED and bend the ends of the wires.

4

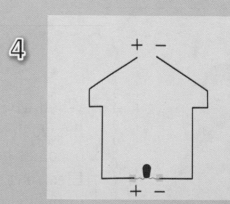

Using a tape, secure the LED upright on the gap at the bottom such that the longer side of the LED wire is aligned with the positive mark and the shorter side is aligned with the negative mark on the drawing. Make sure that the wires are in contact with the lines of your drawing.

5

Now, place a 9V battery on the top gap such that the positive and negative ends of the battery align with the positive and negative lines you have marked.

6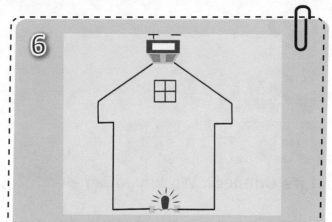

The LED lights up! For best results, you may darken the room and observe the LED glow.

The STEM behind it

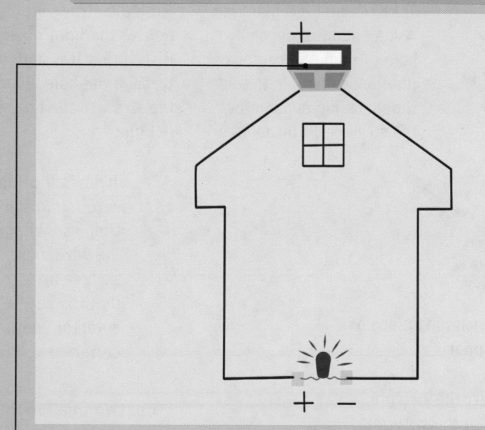

A material can conduct electricity if it has free-flowing electrons in its structure. Graphite is a form of crystalline carbon. The carbon atoms in a graphite molecule have delocalized electrons which are able to move freely in its framework. When we place the battery on the drawing, the free electrons in graphite carry electricity and light up the LED.

52

CHARGE DETECTOR

Life Connect: Working of an electroscope

DIFFICULTY LEVEL

Adult supervision required

You Need

- A clear glass jar with lid
- A straw
- A 14-gauge copper wire
- Scissors
- Pliers or wire cutter
- Aluminum foil
- Hot glue gun
- An inflated balloon

1 Cut a 2-inch long piece of straw using scissors.

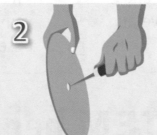

2 Take the lid off a glass jar. Ask an adult to punch a hole through the center of the lid. The hole in the lid should be big enough for the straw to fit through.

3 Push the straw into the hole of the lid. Position it such that it is halfway through the hole. Secure the straw to the lid using hot glue.

4 Using pliers, cut a 10-inch long piece of copper wire from the spool.

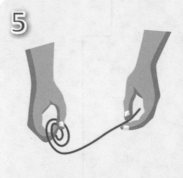

5 Twist half of the wire into a spiral. Doing so will give the wire more surface area so that the charge detector works better.

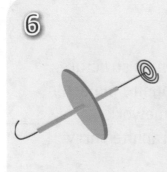

6 Insert the straight end of the wire into the straw such that a portion of the wire hangs out of the straw. Bend the hanging end of the wire and shape it like a hook.

7 Cut two small triangles out of aluminum foil and punch a hole in them. Hang the triangles from the hook of the copper wire such that they are next to each other.

⑧ Screw the lid on the jar. You may also secure it using a piece of tape. Your charge detector is now ready!

⑨ To test it, inflate a balloon and rub it back and forth on your hand or hair for some time. Then, hold the balloon close to the copper spiral at the top of the lid. The aluminum pieces spread apart!

The STEM behind it

When we rub the balloon on our hand or hair, electrons from our hands/hair are transferred to the balloon. The balloon becomes negatively charged and our hands positively charged.

Bringing the balloon close to the copper coil causes the electrons on the coil to move down the tube because like charges repel each other. These electrons are transferred to the aluminum pieces through the hook.

Both pieces of aluminum foil become negatively charged and repel each other.

53
DOES WATER CONDUCT ELECTRICITY?

Life Connect: Testing electrical conductivity of water

DIFFICULTY LEVEL

Adult supervision required

You Need
- A medium-sized container
- A small LED bulb
- Two small button batteries
- Two pieces of electrical wires with alligator clips
- Salt water
- Distilled water
- Tape

1

Fill a medium-sized container with water. Add two spoons of table salt to it. This is your salt water.

2

Connect the alligator clip of one of the electrical wires to one leg of the LED bulb and the clip of the second wire to the second leg of the LED bulb. This makes an open circuit.

3
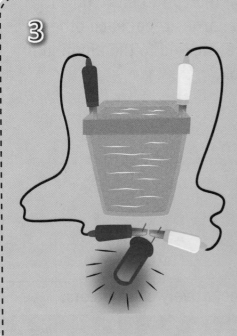

Ask an adult to secure the alligator clips of the two open ends of the wires on the container filled with salt water. Make sure that the alligator clips are slightly dipped in water. Does the LED bulb light up? Yes, it does!

4

Now, fill another container with distilled water.

5 Repeat Step 3 and observe if the LED bulb lights up. Ask yourself why it does not light up the bulb?

The STEM behind it

Pure water is a bad conductor of electricity whereas impure water is an efficient conductor of electricity.

Table salt is made up of sodium and chlorine. When we add salt to water, the water molecules pull the sodium and chlorine ions apart, making them move freely in water. These ions carry electricity from one wire to another through water and the bulb lights up.

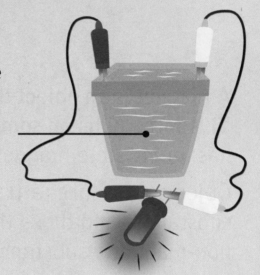

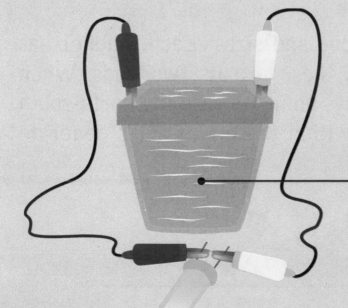

However, since distilled water is pure, it may not contain ions to carry electricity. Hence, the bulb doesn't light up.

EXPERIMENTS WITH

MAGNETS

A magnet is an object that has an invisible force called magnetism. This force pulls on some metals such as iron and nickel. A magnet has an invisible magnetic field around it.

Objects that are attracted to a magnet are called magnetic substances and those that are not attracted to magnets are called non-magnetic substances.

Magnets come in different shapes and sizes. Each magnet has a north pole and a south pole, these are its two ends. When suspended freely, a magnet always points toward the north-south direction. The magnetic forces within these two poles generate the magnetic field.

54
MAKE A FLOATING NEEDLE COMPASS

DIFFICULTY LEVEL

Life Connect: Finding directions using a magnet

You Need
- A sewing needle
- A ruler
- A bar magnet
- Sturdy paper
- Scissors
- Tape
- Water
- A shallow dish

1 Fill a shallow dish with water and keep it aside.

2 Draw a circle of 2-inch diameter on a piece of paper using a compass. Cut it carefully using scissors. This is our circular disk.

3 Secure a sewing needle in the middle of the disk using tape.

4 Now, take the magnet and rub it along the needle in the same direction for around 20-30 times.

5

Slowly place the disk in the shallow dish such that it floats on top. The disk begins to spin around until one end of the needle points towards the north, just like a compass.

The STEM behind it

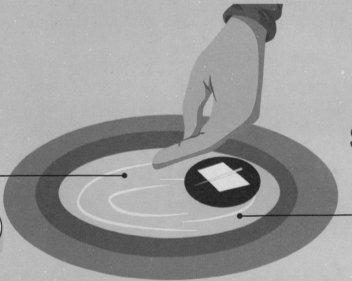

North
Pole

South
Pole

When we place the circular disk in the shallow dish, it floats on the water surface and moves freely. The magnetized needle makes the disk spin around until the north and south poles of the needle are in line with the Earth's magnetic field.

55
MAGNETIC FRUIT

Life Connect: Diamagnetic materials

You Need
- Two large grapes
- A hard drinking straw
- A piece of string around 60 cm long
- Small Neodymium magnets
- Tape
- A ring stand

1

Take a piece of string and tape one of its ends to the middle of the straw.

2

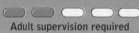

Now, tape the other end of the string to the stand such that the straw can rotate freely like a pendulum.

3

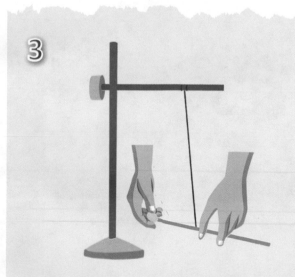

Make a small cut at the stem end of each grape and slide them onto the ends of the straw.

4

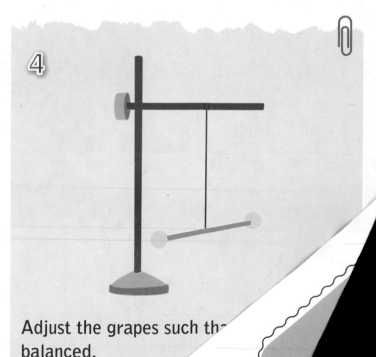

Adjust the grapes such that balanced.

98

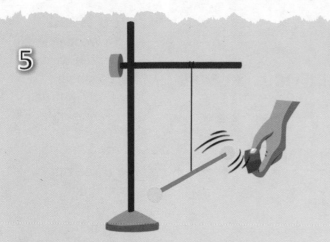

5 Next, hold the north pole of a Neodymium magnet close to one of the grapes. The grape is repelled by the magnet and begins to move away.

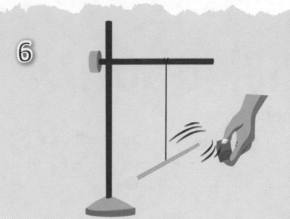

6 Now, turn the magnet and hold the south pole of the magnet close to the grape. This time also, the grape will repel and move away slowly.

The STEM behind it

The grape repelled both the poles of the magnet because of diamagnetism.

When we bring the magnet near the grape, electric current is induced in the atoms of the grape. It turns the grapes magnetic in such a way that they repel the magnet.

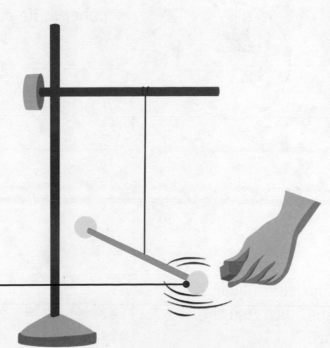

Diamagnetic materials are substances that are usually repelled by magnets. The atoms of such materials contain paired electrons, that is, they pair with electrons of opposite spin. For example, water, helium, bismuth, and graphite. Water is the main component of grapes due to which they show diamagnetism.

56
DANCING DOLL

Life Connect:
Like poles of a magnet repel each other

You Need
- A wooden stand with a wire
- Cardboard
- Cotton thread
- Paper knife
- Tape
- Glue
- Three ring magnets
- Art paper
- Pencil
- Eraser
- Colors

1

Paste an art paper on a piece of cardboard using glue. Then, draw a doll with its feet wide enough to conceal a ring magnet. Color it the way you wish.

2

Now, cut out the doll using paper knife or scissors.

3

Secure a ring magnet horizontally on the doll's feet, using tape, such that the north pole faces outwards.

4

Fix the other two ring magnets on the base of the wooden stand close to where your doll would settle. Arrange the magnets such that their north pole faces outwards.

5 Now, tie a piece of cotton thread to the doll and suspend it from the stand.

6 Swing the doll gently. Does it begin to dance?

The STEM behind it

A magnet has two poles: north and south. When any two magnets are brought together, the unlike poles attract each other while the like poles repel each other.

In this arrangement, the north poles of the magnet located on the doll's feet and the magnets on the wooden stand repel one another, making the doll dance.

57

LED MAGNETS

Life Connect:
Using magnetism to create electricity

DIFFICULTY LEVEL

Adult supervision required

You Need
- Silicon mold tray
- LED light bulbs of different colors
- Button magnets
- Coin cell batteries
- Clear tape
- Hot glue gun

(Note: The number of LEDs, magnets and coin magnets will depend on the number of molds.)

1 Squeeze hot glue into the molds of the silicon tray until it reaches the top. Set it aside until the glue is almost dry, except at the center of the mold where it should be soft and wet.

2 Gently place an LED bulb at the centre of each mold such its back does not sink.

3 Wait for some time until the hot glue dries completely and is cool. Then, carefully pop the molded pieces out of the tray.

4 Now, spread the wires of the LED a little apart and bend them to one side as shown.

5

In each molded piece, secure the button magnet on the wire farthest from the bulb using hot glue.

6

Place the coin battery between the two wires, as shown. Then, tape it to both the wires firmly. Make sure that the longer wire is taped to the positive side of the coin battery.

7

The LED magnets will glow in no time! Detach the battery to turn off the lights.

The STEM behind it

Here, the magnetic field of the magnet helps to generate electricity.

When the coin battery is placed between the wires, the changing magnetic field around the magnet makes the electrons in the wire move, generating an electric current. This makes the LEDs light.

58

ELECTROMAGNETIC TRAIN

Life Connect: Electromagnets

DIFFICULTY LEVEL

You Need
- A roll of 20-gauge copper wire
- An AAA battery
- 6 neodymium magnets of 12 mm diameter each
- 1/2-inch diameter wooden dowels
- Tape

1

Tape one end of the copper wire to a wooden dowel. Slowly, spin the dowel to create a coil of wire, as shown. Make sure the coils are tightly packed and do not overlap.

2

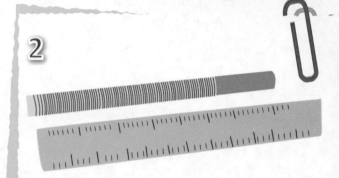

Keep winding the wire until the coil is about 6 in long.

3

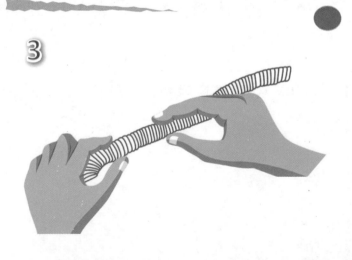

Carefully remove the coil from the dowel. Stretch it gently with your hands such that the loops on the coil do not touch each other.

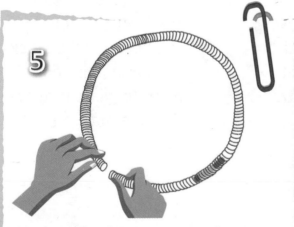

4

Arrange two stacks of three neodymium magnets. Position the stacks such that they repel each other. Now, stick one stack to each end of the battery. Your train is ready!

5

Now, slide the train into the copper coil. It should zip down the coil and out of the other side in no time!

The STEM behind it

The magnetic push moves the train!

When you place the train i.e., the magnet and battery arrangement into the copper coil, it creates a circuit. Electricity from the positive end of the battery moves through the magnets into the copper wire and spirals back to the negative end of the battery.

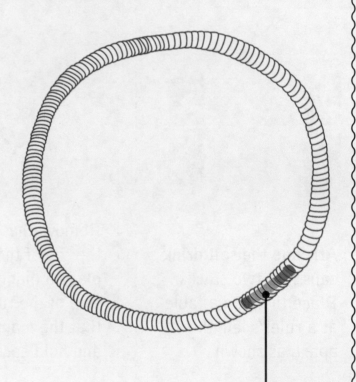

This electricity creates a magnetic field which pushes against the magnets, which in turn pushes the train forward!

59
LET'S BALANCE NUTS

Life Connect: Temporary magnets

DIFFICULTY LEVEL

Adult supervision required

You Need
- 4 full soft drink cans
- 2 ceramic magnets
- A big wooden ruler
- 5 hex nuts
- A tall and heavy drinking glass

1

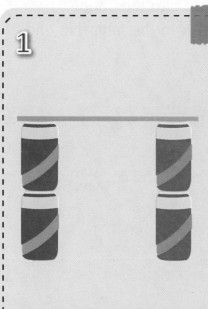

Arrange the soft drink cans into two stacks. Place them on a table at a ruler's length apart, as shown.

2

Remove the ruler from the top of the cans. Now, place a magnet on either side of the ruler such that the magnets attract and hold each other.

3

Place the ruler back on the stacks. Now, keep a drinking glass on the table between the stacks such that a point on the rim of the glass is aligned below the magnets.

4

Now, attach the hex nuts in a hanging column to the magnet underneath the ruler. Position the nuts as straight as you can.

5 Slowly, lower the hanging column of nuts and balance it on the rim of the glass. Make sure that when the nuts are placed on the rim of the glass, they are directly below the magnet on the ruler.

6 You shall see the hex nuts balanced on the rim of the glass.

The STEM behind it

The hex nuts behave as temporary magnets and hold each other in place.

When we attach one hex nut under another to the magnet, they develop an internal magnetic field of their own. The magnetic field (though weak) works even when the nuts are detached from the magnet and placed on the rim of the glass. Thus, they remain balanced on the glass.

60
LENZ'S LAW AND GRAVITY

Life Connect: Lenz's Law

You Need
- Two copper pipes
- A metal and a magnetic ball of the same size
- A friend or adult to assist

1

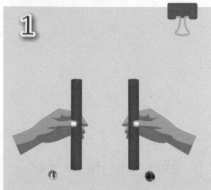

Hold a copper pipe in one of your hands and have a friend hold the other pipe.

2

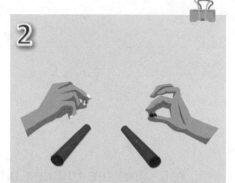

Take the metal ball in the other hand and ask your friend to hold the magnetic ball.

3

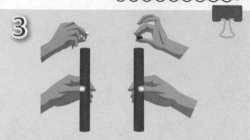

Drop the metal ball through the copper pipe and have your friend drop the magnetic ball through the pipe she/he holds. Make sure that both the balls are dropped at the same time.

4

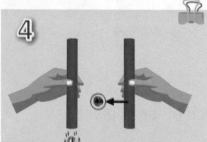

Note the time the balls take to fall through the pipe. The metal ball falls before the magnetic ball.

5

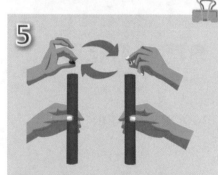

Now, swap the balls and drop them through the pipes again.

6

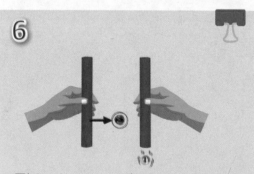

This time too the metal ball falls before the magnetic ball.

The STEM behind it

When you drop the magnetic ball through a copper pipe, its changing magnetic field induces an electric current in the pipe. This current flows in the direction opposite to the moving magnet. This exerts a force on the magnet and slows it down.

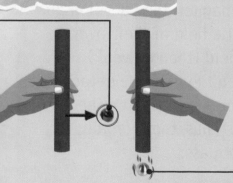

The metal ball does not experience these forces and thus falls before the magnetic ball.

61
SEPARATING MIXTURES

Life Connect: Magnetic substances

You Need
- A cup of sand
- A cup of iron filings
- A bar magnet
- A shallow plate

1 Pour a cup of iron filings onto a shallow plate. Then, pour a cup of sand to the same plate.

2 Mix them well with your fingers. Make sure the iron filings and sand are completely mixed.

3 Bring a bar magnet close to the plate. The iron filings are attracted to the magnet leaving the sand behind.

The STEM behind it

Iron is a magnetic substance whereas sand is non-magnetic. Hence, iron filings stick to the magnet separating sand from it.

EXPERIMENTS WITH

COLORS

Colors are an indispensable part of our world. An object appears to be of a certain color because of the way it reflects light. For example, when white light falls on an apple, it absorbs all the colors of light except red. This red light is then, reflected and the apple appears red.

Red, blue, and yellow are primary colors. Other colors such as green, orange, brown, etc., are secondary colors which are formed by mixing primary colors in different combinations.

62

COLOR PATTERNS

DIFFICULTY LEVEL

Life Connect: Printing in color

You Need
- Poster colors
- A paintbrush
- A palette
- A rectangular sheet of thick white paper
- A shallow glass dish
- Linseed oil

1

Put different poster colors onto the palette.

2

Pour some linseed oil over each color and mix it well using a brush.

3

Take a shallow dish and fill it half with water. Now, dip a paintbrush in one color and gently add the paint to the water in the dish.

4

Similarly, add the other colors one by one. Then, gently swirl the colors with the brush to create a pattern.

5

Place a sheet of thick white paper on the surface of the water in the dish.

6

Slowly remove the paper from the water and let it dry on a table.

7

When the paper dries, you can see beautiful color patterns on it.

The STEM behind it

When we add the mixture of color and oil to the dish, it does not dissolve with water and floats on the surface.

Later, when we place the sheet of paper on the water, the colored oil transfers onto it, forming beautiful patterns.

63

SKITTLES

Life Connect:
Diffusion and water stratification

DIFFICULTY LEVEL

You Need
- A packet of skittles
- A cup of warm water
- A shallow white plate

1

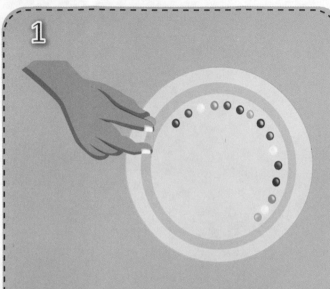

Take a white plate and arrange the skittles in a row around the edge of the plate as shown.

2

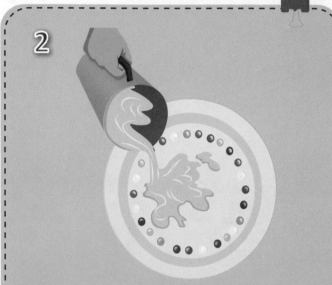

Carefully pour warm water onto the center of the plate such that all the skittles are covered.

3

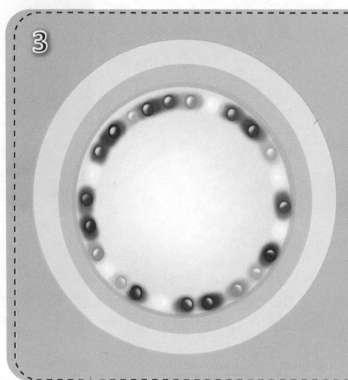

Wait for some time and watch what happens.

④

You will observe that the color of the skittles slowly spreads out toward the center of the plate but they do not mix.

The STEM behind it

The coating on skittles mostly comprises of sugar and food coloring. When we pour warm water onto the plate, it causes the sugar and coloring to diffuse in water.

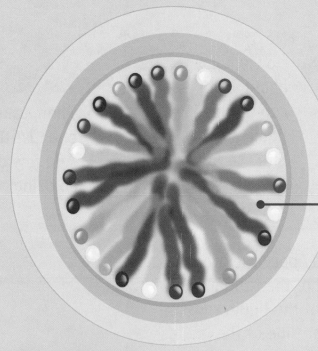

The colors do not mix because of a property called water stratification. When the food coloring from different skittles diffuses in warm water, they create a water solution with slightly different properties. This prevents the colors from mixing.

64

MAKE A RAINBOW

DIFFICULTY LEVEL

Life Connect: Density

1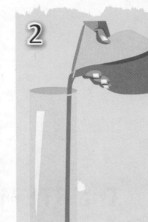

Take a small jar and pour 1/4th cup honey into it. Then, add a drop of red and blue food coloring into it and stir well. You now have a purple colored mixture.

2

Pour the purple mixture carefully into a tall jar.

3

Next, slowly pour about 1/4th cup of blue liquid soap into the tall jar.

4

Then, take a drinking glass and pour 1/4th cup of water into it. Add few drops of green food coloring to it and mix well.

5

Carefully pour the green liquid into the tall jar such that the liquid runs down the side of the jar. Place the jar on a table and allow the liquids to settle.

6

Now, tilt the tall jar again and pour about 1/4th cup of olive oil into it. The colors should not mix.

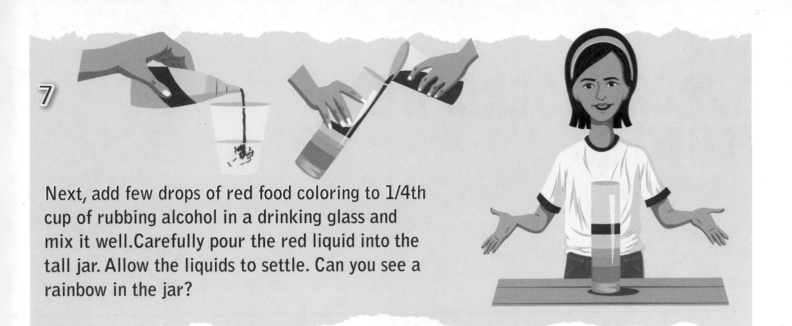

7

Next, add few drops of red food coloring to 1/4th cup of rubbing alcohol in a drinking glass and mix it well. Carefully pour the red liquid into the tall jar. Allow the liquids to settle. Can you see a rainbow in the jar?

The STEM behind it

The arrangement of liquids in the tall jar resemble a rainbow due to the difference in the density of liquids.

Water, olive oil, and alcohol are layered from heaviest to lightest from the bottom, giving the rainbow its distinct lines.

Liquid soap is lighter than honey but heavier than olive oil, so it settles next.

Honey has the highest density among all the liquids so it settles at the bottom.

65

CHROMATOGRAPHY FLOWERS

Life Connect: Paper chromatography

DIFFICULTY LEVEL

You Need
- Filter paper
- A pencil
- Scissors
- Water-based markers
- Tape
- Water
- A medium-sized plastic cup
- A cloth towel
- A straw

1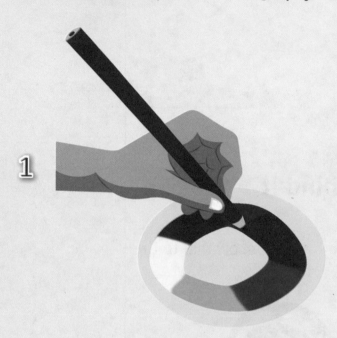

Take a circular filter paper and make a pattern using water-based markers. Try to use dark colors.

2

Take a medium-sized plastic cup and a pour little water into it.

3

Gently place the filter paper circle into the cup such that its middle part touches the water. Wait for around five minutes. You will find the ink of different markers spreading on the paper.

4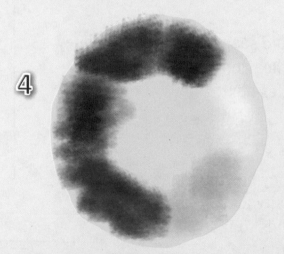

Now, remove the colored filter paper from the cup and place it on a towel to dry.

5

Once the paper is dry, fold it into fourths and cut off the top in the shape of a petal.

6

Open up the filter paper and attach it to a straw using tape.

7

Roll the paper into a flower shape and tape it to the straw at the bottom. Your chromatography flower is ready.

The STEM behind it

Paper chromatography is the technique behind it. Water moves up the filter paper due to a process called capillary action.

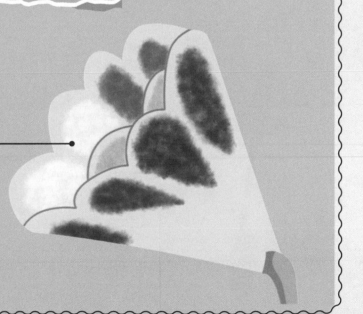

As the water moves up the paper, the ink from the markers dissolves in it. This dissolved ink also moves with the water and spreads out on the paper, coloring it.

66 COLOR CHANGING WATER

Life Connect: Primary and secondary colors

DIFFICULTY LEVEL

1

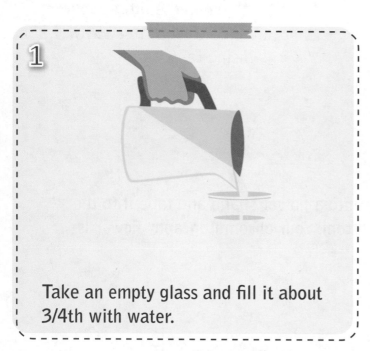

Take an empty glass and fill it about 3/4th with water.

2

Squirt a few drops of blue food colouring into water. Mix the food coloring properly and keep it aside.

3

Next, take an empty jug and fill it with water. Add a few drops of yellow food coloring to it and mix it properly.

4

Get a large glass bowl. Now, carefully place the glass with blue water in the middle of the bowl.

5 Pour some yellow water from the jug into the bowl around the glass. Pour carefully so that the yellow water doesn't get into the glass with blue water.

6 Now, look through the side of the bowl. Do you see another color beside blue and yellow?

The STEM behind it

The water in the glass appears green when we look through the bowl.

Red, yellow, and blue are primary colors. When these three colors are combined together in equal amounts, they make white light. However, when we combine these colors in different amounts, other colors are formed. These colors are called secondary colors.

When we look at the two colors (yellow and blue) at once, the colors mix and the water appears green.

KITCHEN

CHEMISTRY

Our kitchens are a great place to study science. From slicing an apple to making sugar syrup, everything in the kitchen involves chemistry. Various processes such as heating, freezing, melting, blending, etc., are involved in various physical and chemical changes that transform the ingredients we use while cooking. We can explore a lot about kitchen science by learning about how these processes work.

67
MAKE A BOUNCY BALL

Life Connect: Polymers

DIFFICULTY LEVEL

Adult supervision required

You Need
- 2 Plastic cups
- One marker pen
- One tablespoon
- One teaspoon
- 100 ml of hot water
- 100 g of corn flour
- 100 ml of PVA glue
- 100 g of Borax
- Food Coloring

1

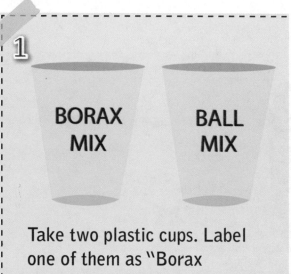

Take two plastic cups. Label one of them as "Borax Mixture" and the other as "Ball Mixture".

2

Add half a teaspoon of borax and two tablespoons of hot water into the cup labelled "Borax Mixture". Then, add a few drops of food coloring and stir until the borax dissolves completely.

3

Now, add about half a teaspoon of the "Borax Mixture" you just made, and one tablespoon of cornflour into the cup labelled "Ball Mixture". Keep it aside for about 15 seconds.

4

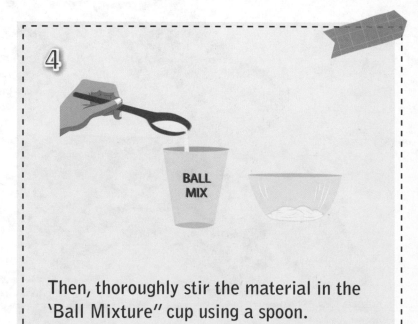

Then, thoroughly stir the material in the 'Ball Mixture" cup using a spoon.

5

Once the mixture becomes thick and is difficult to stir, scoop it out and roll it in your hands. Knead it into the shape of a ball.

6

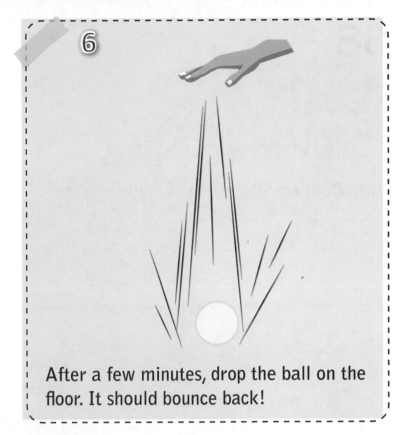

After a few minutes, drop the ball on the floor. It should bounce back!

The STEM behind it

Poly-Vinyl Alcohol is a polymer made up of lots of units added together into long chains. These chains slip and slide past one another, which gives it a liquid structure.

Borax when mixed with Poly-Vinyl Alcohol takes hold of its polymer chains and links them together.

BORAX

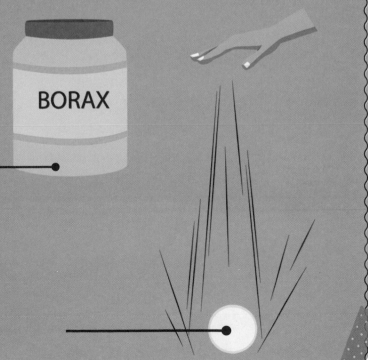

When we add cornflour to the mixture and knead it, the resulting substance becomes harder. It takes the form of a solid combined with an elastic slime! When you hit the ball on the floor, it can then transfer the force back and bounce easily.

68

COLOR CHANGING MILK

Life Connect: Digestion of lipids

DIFFICULTY LEVEL

You Need
- Whole milk
- A shallow plate
- Cotton swabs
- Food coloring (red, yellow, green, blue)
- Dishwashing soap

1

Take a shallow plate and pour some milk onto it. Allow the milk to settle for a few seconds.

2

Add a drop each of red, yellow, blue, and green food coloring to the milk. Make sure the drops are close together in the center of the plate.

3

Take a clean cotton swab and gently place its tip at the center of the milk. Do not stir the milk.

4

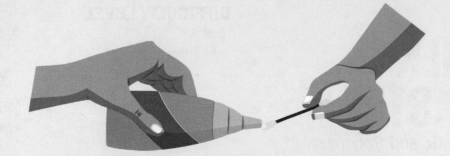

Now, remove the cotton swab from the milk. Dip the other end of the swab in dish-washing soap such that just a drop of it is on the swab.

5

Place the soapy end of the swab in the center of the plate and hold it for about 15 seconds. Do you see a burst of color?

The STEM behind it

Milk contains water, vitamins, minerals, and fats. When we place the soapy end of the cotton swab in the milk, it separates the water and the fat in it. Fat molecules are hydrophobic in nature, i.e., they repel water and bind with the molecules of the dish-washing soap. These bonds are so strong that they push the food coloring around everywhere, resulting in the color explosion.

69
TURN MILK INTO PLASTIC

Life Connect: Plastic and Polymers

1

Pour a cup of milk into a glass kettle and heat it on the hot plate until it is steaming.

2

Pour the milk into a mug. Now, add four teaspoons of white vinegar to it.

3

Stir it with a spoon. Soon, you should see white clumps (solids) formed out of the milk.

4

Carefully, strain the liquid into the kettle with the help of a strainer.

5

Next, place 2-3 paper towels on a tray. Then, scoop out the solids from the strainer onto the towels using a spoon.

6

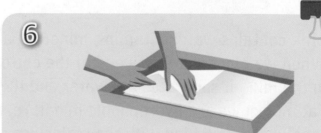

Fold the paper towels over the solids and press them gently to soak up the excess liquid.

7

Add a few drops of food coloring to the solids when they are fairly dry.

8

Knead the solids into a ball of dough.

9

Once the dough is smooth, roll it flat. You can then shape it using cookie cutters.

10

Let the shapes dry for a few days. They will turn into hard plastic.

The STEM behind it

Milk contains a protein called casein. When we added vinegar to hot milk, it curdled and separated into solids and whey. This is because the molecules of casein protein unfold and rearrange into long chains called polymers, which later harden into plastic.

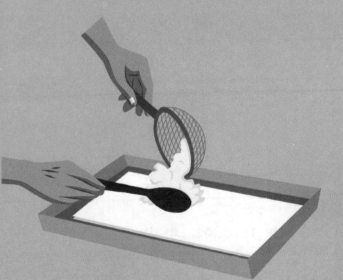

70

METALLIC EGG ILLUSION

Life Connect: Formation of soot

DIFFICULTY LEVEL

Adult supervision required

1

Keep a tripod stand on a table and place a raw egg on it.

2

Then, place a candle below the egg and light it using a lighter.

3

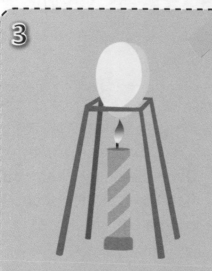

Let the egg char on the flame for some time.

4

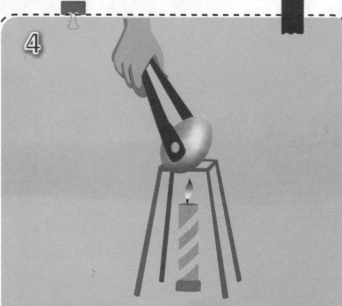

Now, flip the egg carefully on the stand using a pair of tongs. Do this once or twice so that the egg is completely charred from all sides.

5

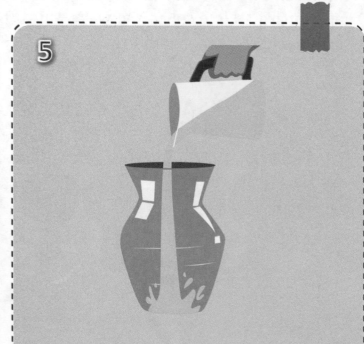

Then, take a glass pitcher and fill it with water.

6 Pick up the egg carefully from the stand and lower it into the pitcher.

7 Observe the egg through the water. The black egg will turn into a metallic egg!

The STEM behind it

When we place the egg over the candle flame, the wax in the candle does not burn completely. This results in the formation of soot, which consists of coal, carbon dioxide, water, and tar.

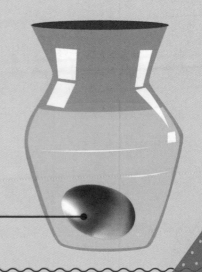

The soot covers the surface of the eggshell. When the egg is placed in water, the layer of soot repels the water in the pitcher. The egg is covered with a thin layer of air, which reflects light and makes the egg look metallic.

71
HOMEMADE pH PAPER

Life Connect: pH indicators

You Need
- A cup of blackberries
- 1/4th cup water
- Dish soap
- Vinegar
- A small bowl
- Two cups
- Scissors
- Thick white paper
- Paper towels
- Ziplock bags

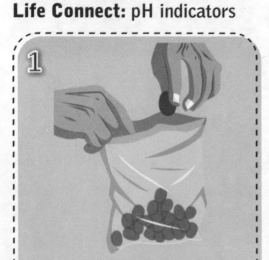

1 Take a ziplock bag and put some blackberries into it.

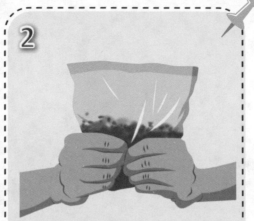

2 Zip up the bag and mash the berries until they are completely crushed.

3 Now, open the ziplock bag and add a little water to the berries. This is just to make the juice thin.

4 Shake the bag two to three times and then pour the berry juice into a bowl. Keep it aside.

5 Next, cut some thin strips out of a thick white paper.

6

Dip these strips in the bowl of berry mush such that they are coated with the juice. Take out the strips and remove any excess juice from them. Place these strips on paper towels and let them dry.

7

Take two small cups. Pour some vinegar into one cup and a mixture of water and dish soap into the other.

8

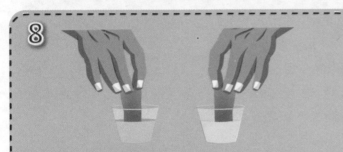

Now, dip half the strip of berry paper into the cups containing the vinegar and dish-soap solution. Wait for 5 minutes. Did you notice a change in the color of the strip?

9

Remove the berry paper strips from the cups and place them on a piece of paper towel to dry.

The STEM behind it

The berry paper strip we had made is a pH indicator. Blackberries, strawberries, and blueberries contain a pigment called anthocyanin, which dissolves in water. This pigment changes color in response to the changing pH levels and can be used to test the pH levels of different substances.

When we dip the berry paper strip in vinegar, it turns pinkish red. When it is dipped in dish-soap solution, it turns deep purple.

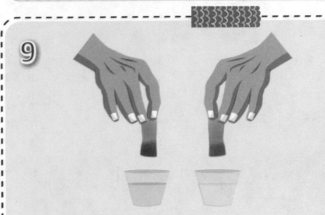

72
CABBAGE JUICE pH INDICATOR

Life Connect: Acids and bases

You Need
- Red cabbage
- A clear jug
- 8-10 clear drinking glasses
- Water
- Blender
- Strainer
- A piece of white paper
- Testing substances- baking soda, lemon juice, hand sanitizer, sugar solution, carbonated drink, bleach, water and vinegar

1

With the help of an adult, cut a portion of red cabbage into thin slices.

2

Put these slices of cabbage into a blender and pour some water in it.

3

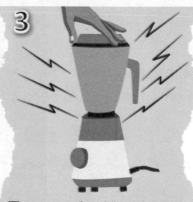

Turn on the blender to blend the cabbage and water until you have reddish-purple cabbage juice.

4

Strain the cabbage juice into a clear jug.

5

Add some water to a clear drinking glass. Now, add some sugar to it.

6

Stir the water with a spoon. This is your sugar solution.

7 Similarly, prepare different solutions by adding your testing substances in clear drinking glasses. Place them in order.

8 Now, pour some cabbage juice into each glass, one by one.

9 Notice the change in the color of each solution. Some of them change into shades of red, while others change into shades of green. Why does that happen?

The STEM behind it

The red cabbage juice is a pH indicator. It changes color when it comes in contact with an acid or a base.

All bases would turn into shades of green when mixed with cabbage juice.

All acids will turn into shades of red.

The darker the shade, the higher the concentration of the acid or the base.

73
ICE CREAM IN A BAG

Life Connect: Freezing Point Depression

DIFFICULTY LEVEL

Adult supervision required

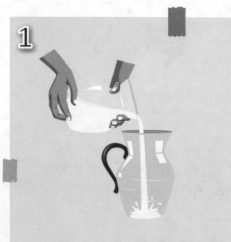

1 Pour a cup of whole milk into a large jug.

2 Add a cup of heavy cream, 2 teaspoons of sugar, a few drops of vanilla extract, and food coloring to it.

3 Stir the mixture with a spoon.

4 Now, carefully pour the mixture into a small ziplock bag and close it completely.

5 Take a large ziplock bag and put about 8-10 ice cubes in it. Cover the ice with a small handful of salt.

6

Put the small ziplock bag with the mixture into the larger ziplock bag as shown. Add more ice and salt until the bag is almost full.

7

Zip the large ziplock bag shut. Now, put on your winter gloves and shake it back and forth for about 5 to 7 minutes.

8

Open the large ziplock bag and take the smaller ziplock bag out. Is it full of ice cream? Scoop it out and enjoy!

The STEM behind it

When we add salt to the ice in the large ziplock bag, it lowers the freezing point of ice by a few degrees. This means that the ice will begin to melt faster than it usually does. In order for the ice to melt further, it needs heat, which in this case is absorbed from the ingredients of the ice cream in the smaller ziplock bag.

74

SEPARATING EGG WHITES AND YOLK

Life Connect: Air pressure

DIFFICULTY LEVEL

Adult supervision required

You Need
- A raw egg
- An empty plastic bottle (preferably water bottle)
- A plate

1

Crack an egg into a plate carefully so that the yolk doesn't break.

2

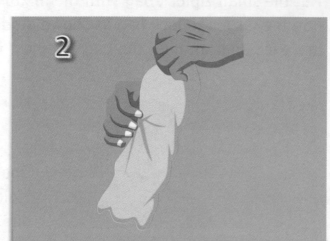

Take an empty plastic bottle and remove its cap. Place one hand on the mouth of the bottle and squeeze it lightly from the middle with your other hand. Be careful not to compress it hard.

3

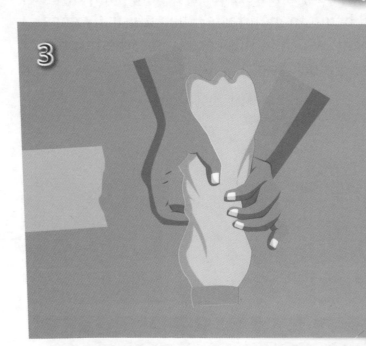

Hold the bottle in the squeezed position without removing your hand from its mouth.

4

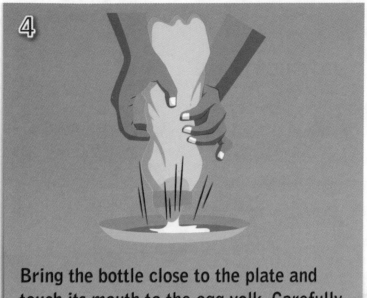

Bring the bottle close to the plate and touch its mouth to the egg yolk. Carefully release the squeeze on the bottle.

5

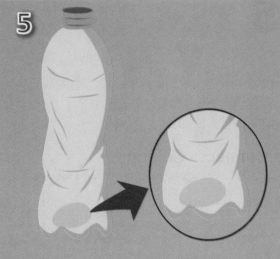

The egg yolk is pushed into the bottle and the egg white is left on the plate.

The STEM behind it

When we squeeze the empty plastic bottle, the pressure of air inside it decreases.

When we release the squeeze on the bottle, air rushes back into the bottle pulling the yolk inside it.

The yolk easily separates from the egg white because of the difference in their viscosity.

75
CANDY IN A JAR

Life Connect: Solutions

You Need
- A pan
- Wooden skewer
- Water
- 2-3 cups of sugar
- A glass jar
- A stirring spoon
- Food coloring
- Scissors
- Clothespin
- A plate

1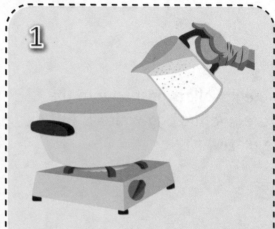

Pour around 250 ml of water into a pan and bring it to a boil.

2

Add about 3 cups of sugar to this hot water and stir it to make a thick solution. Keep adding more sugar and stirring it each time, until no more sugar dissolves in water.

3

Add food coloring to the solution and stir it. Now, allow it to cool.

4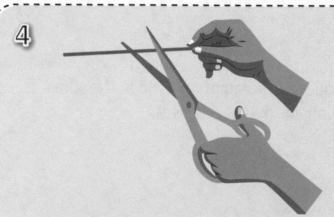

Next, cut a skewer using scissors.

5

Take some sugar in a plate. Dip the skewer in water and roll it in sugar. Let the sugar-coated stick dry for some time.

6

Once the thick sugar solution has cooled down, pour it into a glass jar. Now, clip the clothespin to the sugar-coated skewer and place it in the jar such that it hangs inside the glass, as shown.

7

Place the jar at some place where it will not be disturbed.

8

Wait for around 5-7 days. Observe the changes in the solution every day but do not move it. You should see crystals growing on the skewer. Your sugar candy is ready!

The STEM behind it

When we add sugar to the water, heat and stir it, a supersaturated solution is formed. Such a solution has more dissolved particles of solute that the solvent can hold. The water holds so much sugar because it is hot.

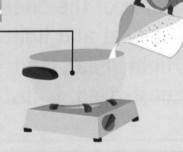

As the water cools down, the sugar particles 'come out' of the solution. They then connect with the sugar particles on the skewer (which acts as seed crystals) and becomes a sugar candy!

EXPERIMENTS WITH

ENERGY

Energy is the ability to do work. It makes everything happen. For example, riding a bike, reading, eating, lighting bulbs, power vehicles, heating homes and various other tasks.

Most of the energy on the Earth comes from the Sun in the form of heat and light. Energy exists in different forms such as sound, light, heat, and electricity. Energy can neither be created nor destroyed. It just changes from one form to another.

76
BALLOON HOVERCRAFT

Life Connect: Newton's third law of motion

DIFFICULTY LEVEL

Adult supervision required

You Need
- A throw-away CD
- A large balloon
- Hot glue gun
- Scissors
- Sap (with pop-up nozzle)

1 Place the CD on a smooth, wooden table with the shiny side up. Now, glue the bottom of the water bottle cap onto the CD such that the hole in the CD and the cap are aligned.

2 Let the glue dry and set properly. Then, press the bottle cap down so that the valve is shut inside the lid.

3 Blow up a balloon and pinch its neck to prevent the air from escaping. Then, carefully attach it to the bottle cap on the CD.

4 The air should not rush out of the balloon while attached to the cap.

5 Open the bottle cap, untwist the balloon, and push the CD a little. Whoooossssh! You can see the balloon hovercraft glide on the table.

The STEM behind it

When we open the bottle cap, air from the balloon shoots down through the hole in the CD and pushes onto the table. This reduces friction between the CD and the table, and at the same time creates an opposite force upwards.

Due to the circular shape of the CD, this force is evenly spread along the bottom of the hovercraft. Thus, the hovercraft glides on the table.

77 SPINNING PENNY

DIFFICULTY LEVEL

●—●—○—○—○

You Need
- A clear balloon
- A coin or a hex nut

Life Connect: Centripetal force

1

Slip a coin through the mouth of a deflated balloon. Make sure the coin is all the way inside the body of the balloon, to prevent any danger of ingesting it while inflating it.

2

Ask an adult to blow up the balloon and tie it with an overhead knot.

3

Hold the balloon at the stem end, as shown. Then, swirl it in a rapid, circular motion. Soon, you shall see the penny spin around the walls of the balloon. It could continue to spin for about 20-30 seconds. Can you hear a lot of noise while it spins?

The STEM behind it

When we move the balloon in a circular motion, the coin climbs up the inside of the balloon.

The shape of the balloon creates a circular path for the coin to move. This allows the coin to spin on its edge while in motion due to the centripetal force—a force that pulls objects toward the center in a circular motion.

78
INSEPARABLE BOOKS

Life Connect: Frictional force

1
Place two same-sized notebooks on a table such that their bindings face inward.

2
Overlap their covers, as shown.

3
Carefully, place pages from each notebook one over the other to intertwine them.

4
Continue until the notebooks are entirely intertwined.

5 Have a friend hold one of the notebooks from the binding, while you hold the other. Now, pull the notebooks and try to separate them. It's difficult! Right?

The STEM behind it

It is friction that holds the books together like glue!

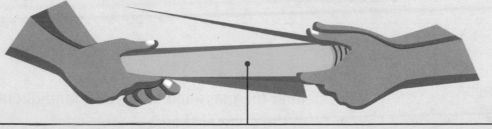

When we pull the books, each sheet of paper produces a small frictional force, which is hardly noticeable. However, this force is multiplied due to the number of pages in the book and we end up with a strong force that prevents us from pulling the books apart.

79

EGG DROP INERTIA

Life Connect: Newton's first law of motion

DIFFICULTY LEVEL

You Need
- A large egg
- A cardboard roll (from toilet paper roll)
- A metal pie pan
- Water
- A large drinking glass
- A jug

1

Fill a clear drinking glass about three-quarters with water.

2

Place a metal pie pan on top of the glass such that it is positioned at the center.

3

Now, place the cardboard roll vertically on the pan, as shown. Make sure it is also positioned at the center.

4

Carefully set the egg horizontally on top of the cardboard roll.

5

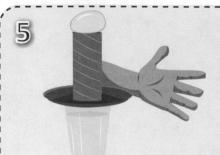

Stand behind the glass and hold your hand about six inches away from the edge of the pan.

6

With a swift and quick motion, hit the side of the pan horizontally. The force should be just enough to push the pan off the glass.

7

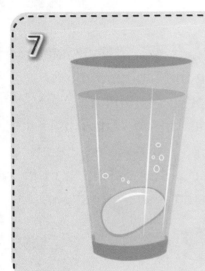

The egg falls directly into the glass. Wasn't that amazing?

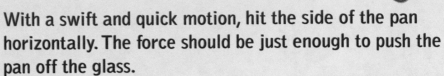
The STEM behind it

The egg falls into the glass due to inertia. The egg placed on top of the cardboard roll is in a state of rest.
When we apply force to the pan, it zips out from under the cardboard roll.

Due to the law of inertia, the egg remains at rest. There is no other force to change its direction except gravity, which pulls it down into the glass.

80

DRIPPING BOTTLE

Life Connect:
Air pressure and Gravity

You Need
- 1 ltr clear plastic bottle with cap
- A sharp pushpin
- Water

1

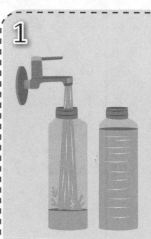

Clean a 1 ltr plastic bottle and fill it with water to the top.

2

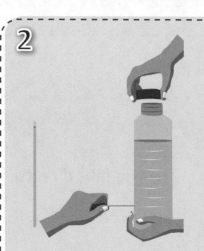

Place one of your hands on the mouth of the bottle and the other at the bottom. Then, have an adult poke a hole at the bottom of the bottle using a sharp pushpin.

3

You will observe that water squirts out of the hole at the bottom.

4

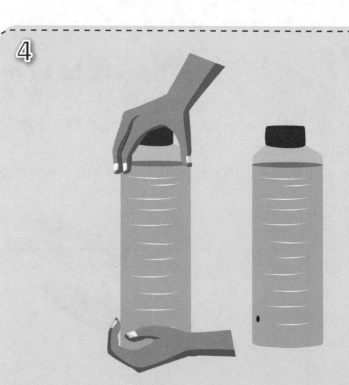

Now, place your finger on the hole and twist the cap to close the bottle. Remove your finger from the hole. Does the water squirt out?

5 Now, open the cap of the bottle. Water pours out from the hole again!

The STEM behind it

When we cover the cap of the bottle, water is pulled down but there is a lack of air pressure inside the bottle. However, air pushes on the outside of the bottle from all sides. Since air pressure in the bottle is lower than it is outside, water stays inside the bottle.

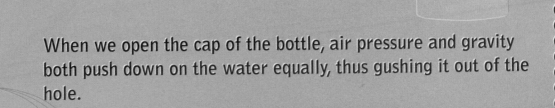

When we open the cap of the bottle, air pressure and gravity both push down on the water equally, thus gushing it out of the hole.

81

MARBLE ROLLER COASTER

Life Connect: Potential and Kinetic Energy

DIFFICULTY LEVEL

Adult supervision required

You Need

- A 4 ft long foam pipe insulation with 1.5-inch diameter
- A glass marble
- Masking tape
- A knife
- A chair or table
- An adult helper

1

With the help of an adult, cut the pipe insulation in half lengthwise so as to form two U-shaped channels.

2

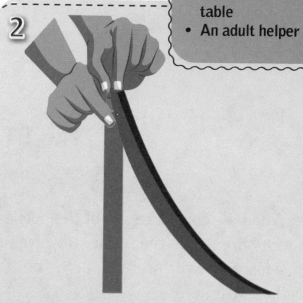

Tape one end of the pipe insulation to a chair.

3

Hold the pipe in place and tape it to the floor, forming a hill. Make sure the tape does not block the inside of the tube.

4

Bend the second pipe insulation into one or two loops. Then, tape it to the floor on both sides of the loops.

5

Now, place a marble a few inches from the bottom of the hill. Does it go all the way through the loop? No! Move the marble a few inches up the track and try again. This time too it does not make it through the loop.

6

Now, place the marble on top of the hill and release it. The marble goes all the way through the loop this time!

The STEM behind it

When we place the marble a few inches from the bottom of the hill, it has little potential energy. Hence, when rolled, it does not make it through the loop.

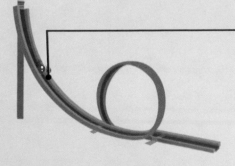

On placing the marble on top of the hill, it has maximum potential energy (and almost no kinetic energy) because it is high off the ground.

As the marble rolls down the hill, this potential energy is converted into kinetic energy (the energy of motion) and the marble rolls down very fast making it through the loop.

82

BALANCING STRUCTURES

Life Connect: Center of gravity

DIFFICULTY LEVEL

○ ○ ○ ○ ○

Adult supervision required

You Need

- A carrot
- 4–5 wooden skewers
- Marshmallows
- A balloon
- Small plastic bottle caps
- A 500 ml plastic bottle
- A sharp pushpin
- Scissors
- Knife

1

With the help of an adult, cut a 3 cm long piece out of a wooden skewer.

2

Then, cut a 3 cm long piece of carrot. Have an adult push a piece of skewer into one end of the piece of carrot.

3

Fill a 500 ml plastic bottle with water and close its lid. Keep the bottle on a table. Now, place the skewer with the piece of carrot on the lid of the bottle and try to balance it. It is very difficult!

4

Next, have an adult push two skewers into each side of the carrot such that they point downward at an angle of 45°.

5

Push a marshmallow onto the ends of the skewers, as shown.

6  Place this on top of the bottle now. You will observe that it balances on the bottle.

7  Now, push 2-3 more skewers into the carrot. Add more objects to the skewers such as a bottle cap, inflated balloon, etc.

8  Place the structure on the bottle to balance it all the way!

The STEM behind it

An object can be balanced if its center of gravity remains in the same vertical line as the point at which it is pivoted.

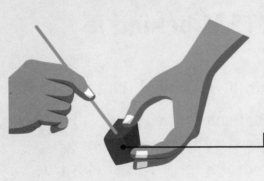

When we place the skewer with only the piece of carrot fixed to it, its center of gravity is not in the same vertical line as the point at which the skewer sits on the bottle.

Placing the complete structure on the bottle brings the center of gravity below the point where the skewer (with the carrot piece) sits on the bottle, thus balancing it.

83

IT'S A FREE FALL

DIFFICULTY LEVEL

Life Connect:
Law of free fall and air resistance

1

Take one of the balloons and fill it with water such that it weighs approximately 250 grams.

2

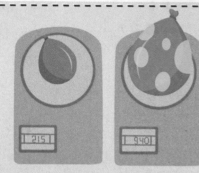

Next, take another balloon and fill it with water such that it weighs four times the first balloon.

3

Now, drop both the balloons from the same height, at the same time. Did the lighter balloon hit the ground before the heavier balloon or did both balloons hit the ground at the same time?

The STEM behind it

Both the balloons hit the ground at the same time!

When we drop the balloons, gravity pulls them down. While pulling objects, gravity causes them to accelerate at a rate of 9.8 m/s². This stands true for all falling objects irrespective of their mass, unless the object is affected by air resistance.

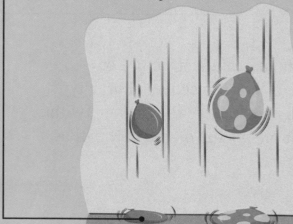

84

SOLAR OVEN

Life Connect: Solar Energy

You Need
- A cardboard pizza box
- A utility knife
- Aluminum foil
- Clear tape
- Black construction paper
- A ruler
- A pencil
- A skewer
- A thick plastic wrap
- A thermometer
- Glue
- Marshmallows

1

Draw a square about 5 cm from the edges on the outside lid of a pizza box.

2
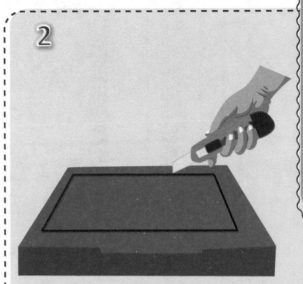

Cut along the square from three sides, using a utility knife. Do not cut along the hinged side of the lid.

3
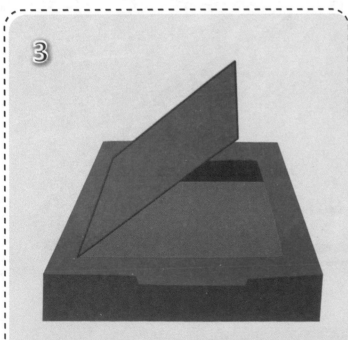

Fold along the uncut side of the square such that it becomes a flap.

4
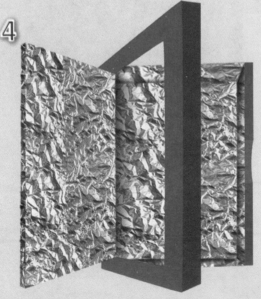

Cut a piece of aluminium foil, big enough to cover the bottom, two sides and inner side of the flap. Wrap the foil around these parts and secure it with tape.

6

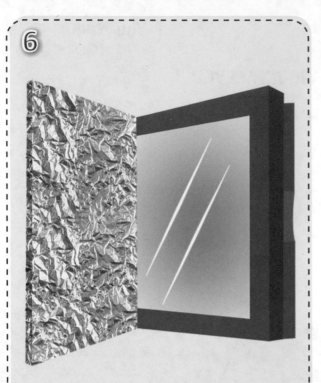

Cover the inside of the box lid with plastic wrap. Make sure the flap can move freely.

7

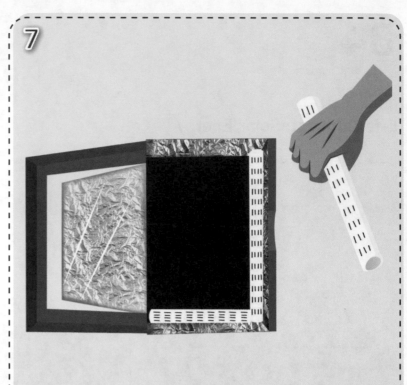

Roll up sheets of newspaper and place them at the bottom of the box. Your solar oven is ready.

5

Next, cut a piece of black construction paper and cover the bottom of the pizza box.

8

Use a skewer to prop the flap of the oven from the rest of the box.

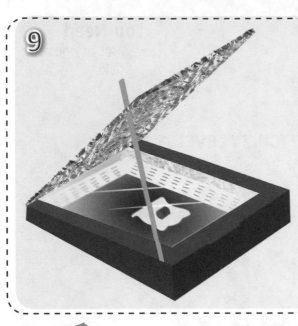

9

Take the oven into the Sun between 11 am and 2 pm. Place the marshmallows on a small square of aluminium foil and put it on the black paper inside your solar oven. Let the oven be in sunlight for around 40 minutes and watch what happens.

The STEM behind it

The flap covered with aluminum foil reflects the sunlight into the oven.

The black construction paper at the bottom of the oven absorbs the Sun's heat. This heats the air inside the oven.

Securing the plastic wrap over the opening in the flap made the oven airtight. Due to this, the warm air inside the oven could not escape from the box.

85
POPSICLE STICK CHAIN REACTION

Life Connect:
Potential and Kinetic Energy

You Need
• A lot of popsicle sticks

DIFFICULTY LEVEL

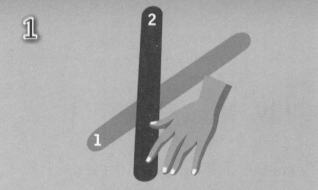

Lay a red and green popsicle stick on a hard, flat surface such that they form an X-shape. Mark them as 1 and 2.

Now, add a green popsicle stick over stick 2 such that it is parallel to stick 1.

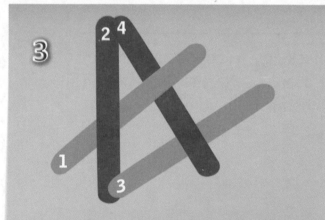

Now add another red stick (stick 4) and tuck it under stick 1 such that one of its ends lays over stick 3 and the rest of it lays over stick 1. Ask an adult to hold on to the end of the chain where you are working.

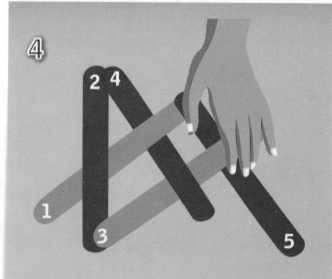

Place a red stick (stick 5) under stick 3. Sticks 4 and 5 should be parallel to each other.

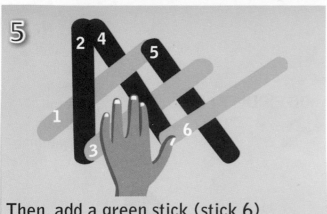

5 Then, add a green stick (stick 6) such that one of its ends is over stick 4.

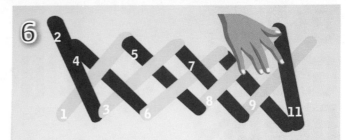

6 Repeat steps 4 and 5 until you have about 15-20 sticks in a chain. Remember, it's an over-then-under arrangement of sticks to hold the chain together.

7 Once you have built the chain, let go of the end of stick 1. The sticks will fall down the line in a chain reaction.

The STEM behind it

As we weave the popsicle sticks into a pattern, one stick is bent over another stick at one end and held under yet another stick on the other end. Due to this, lots of potential energy is slowly built up in the popsicle sticks.

When we let go of the chain, the potential energy is converted into kinetic energy, creating a colorful flair.

GRAVITY DEFYING BEADS

Life Connect: Gravity

DIFFICULTY LEVEL

Adult supervision required

You Need
- A long string of beads
- A tall plastic container

1 Place a tall plastic container on a flat surface. Then, find the end of a string of beads and carefully lay it at the bottom of the container.

2 Layer the string neatly in circles, one on top of the other inside the container. Make sure they are not tangled.

3 Once the beads are loaded, pick up the container in one hand and quickly pull the other end of the string downward. The string of beads will propel itself out of the container in no time!

The STEM behind it

Inertia and gravity make the beads propel out of the container after the initial tug.

When we quickly pull the end of the string downward, we initiate a motion in it. The string now cannot change momentum because no other force is acting upon it except gravity that pulls it down!

HEATING WITH GREENHOUSE EFFECT

Life Connect: Greenhouse effect

DIFFICULTY LEVEL

Adult supervision required

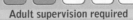

1

Lay the thermometers in a work area with direct sunlight. Set the stopwatch timer to five minutes. After five minutes have passed, read the temperatures displayed on both thermometers. They should read the same.

2

Now, place one of the thermometers inside the glass jar and close its lid. Place it next to the other thermometer. Make sure both the thermometers are fully exposed to the sun.

3

Let the thermometers stay in the sun for about 15-20 minutes. Note the temperatures on both the thermometers every 10 minutes. Did the temperatures change? Are they still the same?

The STEM behind it

As long as both the thermometers are placed in the work area with direct sunlight, they should show the same temperature.

When we place one of the thermometers inside the glass jar, we create an artificial environment for it.

Glass does not allow heat radiation to pass through it. Hence, the heat that is generated from the sunlight inside the jar is unable to escape. Because the heated air inside the jar is trapped, the flow of air stops. Due to this, warm air cannot mix with cold air to cool it down. As a result, the temperature inside the glass jar increase over time.

HANDS-ON

SCIENCE

Hands-on science is all about doing, observing, asking questions, and exploring. Let us carry out some experiments that puts science into application and learn from them. By performing these experiments, we can understand the gaps between theory and practice, and enrich our learning.

88
LET'S MAKE SLIME

Life Connect:
Non-Newtonian Fluid

DIFFICULTY LEVEL

Adult supervision required

1

Mix one tablespoon of borax and 250 ml water in a bowl so that the borax dissolves completely in water.

2

Add a sufficient quantity of glue in a large bowl. Pour water into the bowl. The amount of water should be the same as the amount of glue.

4

Add a few drops of food coloring to it. Mix it thoroughly so that the color spreads evenly.

3

Mix it with your hands until both ingredients are blended properly.

5

Slowly, add the water and borax mixture into the bowl of glue and water mixture and keep mixing. If the slime seems dry, add more water and borax mixture.

6

Mix until it reaches a smooth consistency-elastic and flows very slowly. The slime is ready!

The STEM behind it

Slime sometimes feels like a solid and sometimes like a liquid.

The glue we used is made up of identical, repeating molecules called polymers that are cross-linked with each other in a chain.

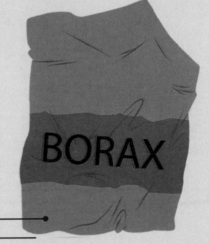

BORAX

When we add the borax and water mixture to the glue, the chemical (sodium tetra borate) in borax links the polymers in it. This forms a putty-like material which we call slime.

89
AIR FRESHENER

Life Connect: Gelatin-based air fresheners

You Need
- A packet of unflavored gelatin
- Water
- Fragrance oil of your choice
- Food coloring
- Table salt
- Small glass jars
- A bowl

1 Add four 20 g packets of gelatin into a bowl and add a cup of boiled water to it.

2 Mix it properly until the gelatin is dissolved in water.

3 Now, add a cup of cold water to the gelatin mixture and stir it well.

4 Then, add one tablespoon of salt to the gelatin mixture. This will keep the mold from growing.

5

Add around 10-20 drops of fragrance oil to the gelatin mixture. You can add a few drops of food coloring as well and stir the mixture. The air fragrance gel is ready.

6

Carefully pour the mixture into a small jar and allow it to set for some time until it turns into a solid. The air freshener is ready to use.

The STEM behind it

Gelatin is a protein derived from collagen. It has a matrix-type structure that allows it to hold its shape.

We add warm water to gelatin because it dissolves in water and changes into a jelly-like structure when it cools.

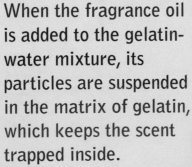

When the fragrance oil is added to the gelatin-water mixture, its particles are suspended in the matrix of gelatin, which keeps the scent trapped inside.

As the gel evaporates, scent particles are released from the matrix, spreading a continuous fragrance of the air freshener.

90
GUMMY BEAR OSMOSIS

You Need
- Two gummy bears of same color and size
- Salt
- Two bowls
- Water

Life Connect:
Osmosis and semi-permeable membranes

1 Place two bowls on a table and pour the same amount of water into each of them. The water should be enough to immerse the gummy bears in this activity.

2 Add salt to one of the bowls of water and stir it well to make a salt solution.

3 Now, record the weight of the gummy bears. Place a gummy bear into each of the bowls and leave them undisturbed for several hours or overnight.

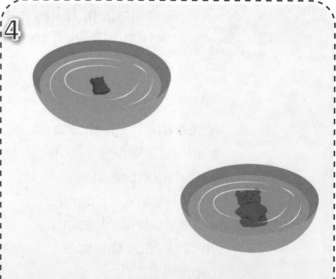

4 Next morning, notice the difference in the gummy bear placed in the salt solution. Record their weights again.

5

The gummy bear kept in the bowl of plain water swells up and becomes bigger in size, and the one placed in the salt solution decreases in volume and mass.

The STEM behind it

The gummy bear swells because of osmosis—a process in which water moves from an area of lower concentration to higher concentration, unless both the concentrations are equal.

Gummybears are made of gelatin and sugar. When the gummy bear is placed in plain water, water moves into it because the concentration of water is higher outside than in the gummy bear. Hence, the gummy bear swells.

The gummy bear in the saltwater shrinks because the concentration of water in the gummy bear is more than that of the salt solution. Water flows from the gummy bear into the salt solution to create an equilibrium.

91

CAPILLARY ACTION

DIFFICULTY LEVEL

Life Connect: Movement of water in plants

You Need
- A celery stalk with leaves attached
- 2 tall, straight drinking glasses
- Water
- Red and blue food coloring
- A knife
- Scissors

1

Cut the bottom of a celery stalk using scissors to freshly expose the xylem. Do it quickly. This will open the tubes of the xylem.

2

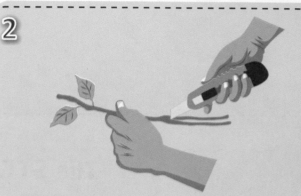

Using a knife, make a vertical slit of about 2-inch at the bottom of the stalk.

3

Next, fill two glasses halfway with water.

4

Pour few drops of red food coloring into one glass and a few drops of blue food coloring into the other glass. Stir them well. Make sure the water in both the glasses has a deep color to get the best effect.

5

Put the two glasses of colored water next to each other. Now, put half of the celery stalk into one glass, and the other half into the second glass, as shown.

6

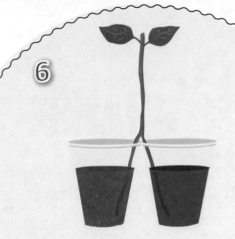

Leave it for a few hours or even overnight. You shall see a change in the color of the stalks.

The STEM behind it

Celery has a number of xylem tubes in its stalk. Xylem tubes are tiny tubes that help a plant draw up water from the roots like a straw. More xylem tubes indicate that more water will be drawn up the stem.

The green leaves of the stalk turn to red and blue because the dissolved food coloring from the glasses moved with the water through the xylem tubes into the celery stalk and leaves.

As the water from the celery leaves evaporates, it deposits the color in the plant. The xylem tubes pull more water and the cycle continues until no water is left in the glasses.

92

WHY DO LEAVES CHANGE COLOR

DIFFICULTY LEVEL

Adult supervision required

Life Connect: Changing color of leaves

You Need

- 2–3 leaves from different plants
- Plastic wrap or aluminum foil
- Rubbing alcohol
- Small glass jars
- Paper coffee filters
- A shallow pan
- Tap water (hot)
- Masking tape
- A plastic spoon

1

Collect 2-3 large leaves from different trees. Cut them into small pieces and put them into two glass jars.

2

Now, add rubbing alcohol into the jars, just enough to cover the leaves. Gently crush the leaves using a plastic spoon.

3

Cover the jars loosely with plastic wrap. Pour some hot water into a shallow tray and place the jars in it.

4

Let the jars stay in the water for at least 30 minutes. Swish the jars very gently every 5 minutes. Also, replace hot water as it cools. You shall notice that the color of the alcohol darkens.

5

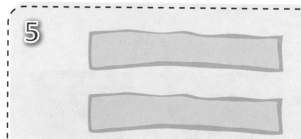

Next, cut long strips out of the paper coffee filter.

6

Remove the jars from water and remove the plasticwraps covering them.

7

Place a strip of filter paper into each jar. Make sure that one of its ends is in the alcohol in the jar and the other end is over the top of the jar. Using a tape, secure the strip to the end of the jar.

8

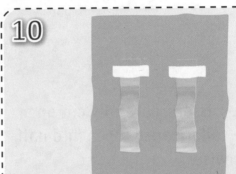

After sometime, you shall observe that the alcohol travels up the paper filter bringing the colors with it.

9

After about 90 minutes, the alcohol starts to evaporate and the colors will travel different distances up the paper. You should see different colors such as green, yellow, etc. on the strips.

10

Remove the strips and allow them to dry. Then, tape them to a piece of paper.

The STEM behind it

Leaves contain a pigment called chlorophyll which gives them their green color. It also contains other colors, but chlorophyll is so dominant that the other colors are hidden.

When we add rubbing alcohol and place the leaves in hot water, the chlorophyll is broken down. The green color became less prominent and other pigments become visible.

93

SHOOT A BALL

Life Connect:
Potential and kinetic energy

DIFFICULTY LEVEL

Adult supervision required

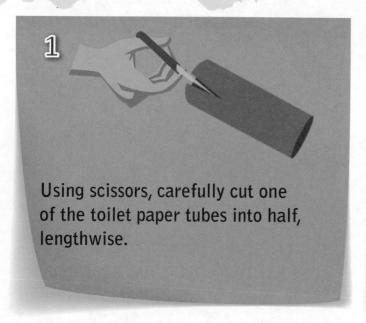

1 Using scissors, carefully cut one of the toilet paper tubes into half, lengthwise.

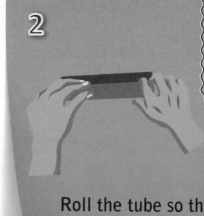

2 Roll the tube so that it is about half the original diameter.

3 Tape the roll to hold it in place.

4 Using a hole puncher, make a hole half an inch away from one of its ends. Make another hole opposite the first hole.

5

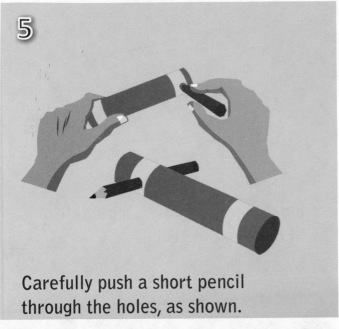

Carefully push a short pencil through the holes, as shown.

6

Next, take the second toilet paper roll and cut two 1/4th inch slits into one end. These slits should be about 1/2 inch apart from each other. Cut two more slits opposite the first two slits. There should be a total of four slits.

7

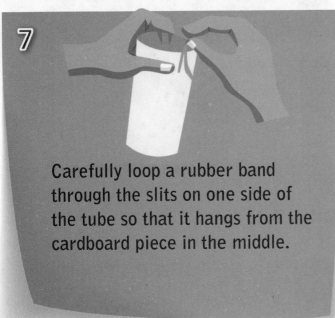

Carefully loop a rubber band through the slits on one side of the tube so that it hangs from the cardboard piece in the middle.

8

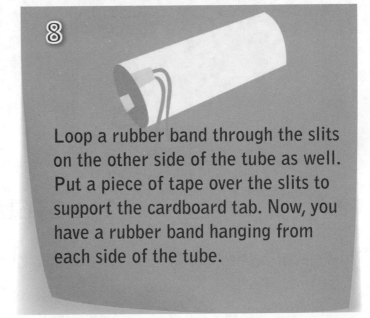

Loop a rubber band through the slits on the other side of the tube as well. Put a piece of tape over the slits to support the cardboard tab. Now, you have a rubber band hanging from each side of the tube.

9

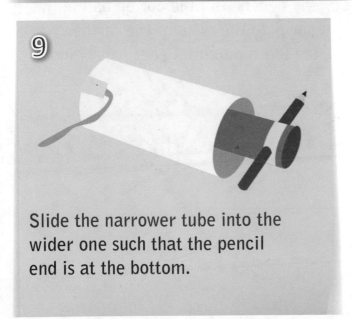

Slide the narrower tube into the wider one such that the pencil end is at the bottom.

10

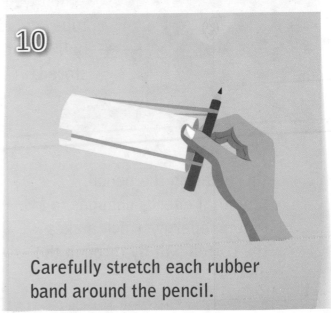

Carefully stretch each rubber band around the pencil.

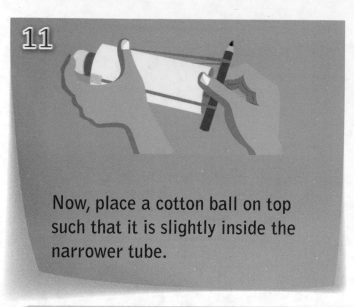

11

Now, place a cotton ball on top such that it is slightly inside the narrower tube.

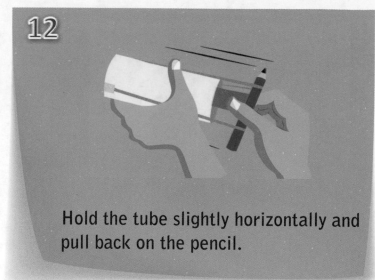

12

Hold the tube slightly horizontally and pull back on the pencil.

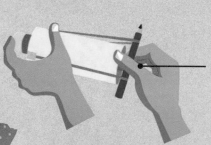

13

Release the pencil and watch the cotton ball fly!

The STEM behind it

The cotton ball launcher is an example of potential energy being converted to kinetic energy.

When we draw back on the pencil with the cotton ball in the tube, we add potential energy to the system. The farther we pull back on the pencil, the more potential energy is being stored.

On releasing the pencil, potential energy changes to kinetic energy, which makes the cotton ball fly through the air!

94
SORTING MACHINE

Life Connect:
Gravity powered sorting machines

DIFFICULTY LEVEL

1

Add a number of large and small marbles into a single plastic cup.

2

Shake the cup so that the marbles are well mixed.

3

Glue several popsicle sticks together to form a grate as shown. Make sure the gaps in the grate are large enough so that the small marbles can pass through them, but small enough so that the large marbles cannot.

4

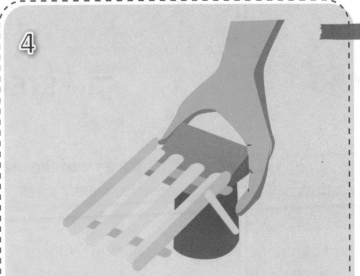

Using plastic cups, popsicle sticks, paper, glue and tape, build a support structure for your grate as shown.

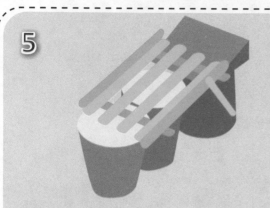

5

Place two cups on a table and place the grate on it. One cup should be placed directly below the grate to collect the smaller marbles as they fall through, and the other cup should be at the lower end of the grate to collect the larger marbles.

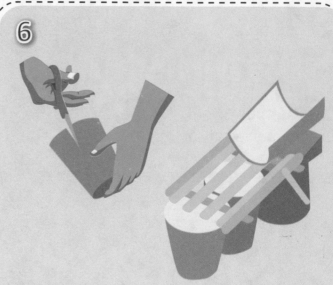

6

Now, carefully cut a plastic cup, and paste it to the grate, as shown. This acts as a funnel at the top end of your grate to pour the marbles into the cups.

7

Pour your cup of mixed marbles into the funnel and watch what happens.

The STEM behind it

When the marbles are poured into the grate at the top, they roll down the popsicle sticks as gravity pulls them down.

The diameter of the smaller marbles is lesser than the gap between the popsicle sticks, hence they fall through the gap into the first cup.

However, the diameter of the larger marbles is more than the gap between the sticks. Thus, they continue rolling to the second cup.

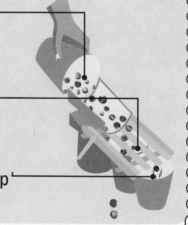

95
PUMPING HEART MODEL

Life Connect:
Working of human heart

DIFFICULTY LEVEL

Adult supervision required

1

Fill a medium-sized glass jar with water. Add a few drops of food coloring to it and mix well.

2

Take a deflated balloon and cut off its neck. Keep the top part aside.

3

Now, stretch the bottom part of the balloon over the mouth of the jar filled with colored water. Secure it with a rubber band. Make sure the balloon is as tight as possible.

4

Using a knife, make two small slits in the balloon such that they are an inch apart. Make sure the slits are small enough to just push the straws in.

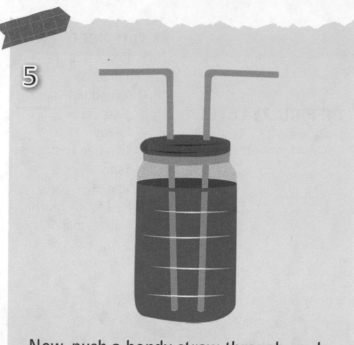

5 Now, push a bendy straw through each of the slits such that the bendy parts are on the top.

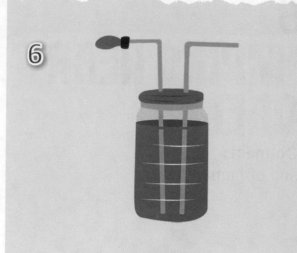

6 Cover the opening of one straw sticking out of the glass jar with the neck of the balloon that you cut in step 2. Secure it with tape.

7 Set the jar in a tray and bend the straw with the open end. Now, press the center of the stretched balloon gently. The colored water pumps out of the bendy straw just as the heart pumps blood.

The STEM behind it

Our heart is made up of four chambers. The top chambers are called atrium and the bottom ones are called ventricles. Each chamber of the heart has valves to control the flow of blood. When the valves open up, blood flows from the top to the bottom chamber and then out of the heart. The valves also prevent blood from flowing back to the atrium.
The glass jar filled with colored water acts as the heart.
The stretched balloon acts as the muscles of the heart.
Pressing the stretched balloon is like the pumping of the heart due to which the colored water (which represents blood) squirts out.
The balloon neck which covers the straw acts as the valve keeping the flow of blood in the right direction.

96

PENDULUM ARTIST

Life Connect:

DIFFICULTY LEVEL

You Need
- A long string
- A 1 ltr plastic bottle
- Acrylic paint
- A sheet of foam rubber
- An awl
- A clamp
- A horizontal crossbar
- Water
- A glass
- Stirring spoon

1

With the help of an adult, cut a plastic bottle into half.

2

Next, using an awl, make two holes in the top half of the bottle. The holes should be opposite to each other. Now, pass a string through the holes.

3

Make a tiny hole in the cap of the bottle. Secure the cap back onto the bottle firmly.

4

Attach a clamp to the string and tie the ends of the string to a straight horizontal crossbar. Observe that the clamp divides the system into two sections such that the upper section can swing only in one direction, while the lower section can swing in all directions. This is your pendulum.

5

Place a sheet of foam rubber under the pendulum.

6

Pour some water into a glass and add some paint to it. Mix it well so that the paint dissolves properly and you have colored water.

7

Now, pull the pendulum to one side and pour some colored water into it.

8

Let go of the pendulum and watch the symmetrical patterns it creates!

The STEM behind it

A pendulum is a load suspended from a fixed point so that it can swing freely in all directions. But in the pendulum we made, the suspension point itself can oscillate. Such a pendulum performs two harmonic oscillations simultaneously and creates beautiful symmetrical patterns.

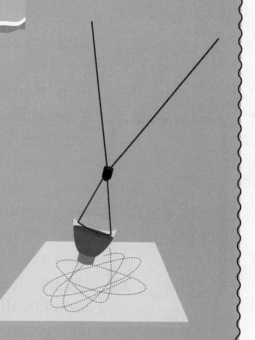

97
STRAWBERRY DNA

Life Connect: DNA extraction

You Need
- A strawberry
- 5 ml Isopropyl alcohol
- 10 ml dish soap
- 1/4th teaspoon salt
- A ziplock bag
- A strainer
- 90 ml water
- Measuring cups and spoons
- A small and a medium glass container
- Tweezers
- A spoon

1

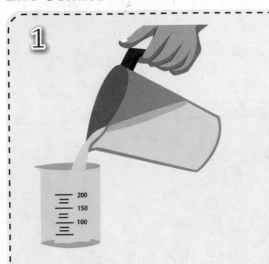

Before beginning the experiment, put a bottle of isopropyl alcohol in a freezer. Pour 90 ml of water into a small glass container.

2

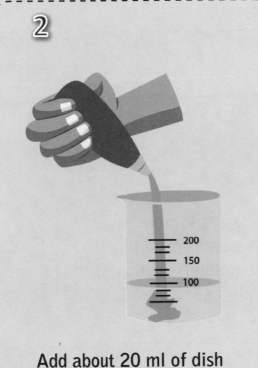

Add about 20 ml of dish soap to the water.

3

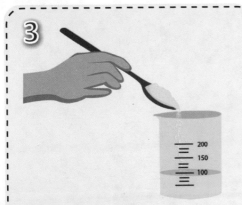

Now, add 1/4-teaspoon salt to the mixture of water and dish soap, and mix until the salt dissolves. This is the extraction mixture.

4

Place one strawberry into a plastic ziplock bag.

5

Slowly, pour the extraction mixture into the ziplock bag with the strawberry.

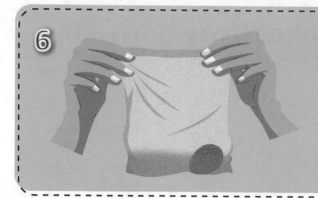

6 Remove air from the bag by pushing it and close its seal.

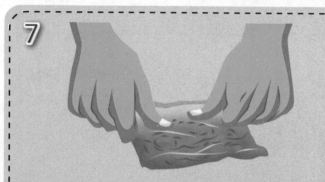

7 Using your hands, mash and smash the strawberry inside the bag. Make sure the strawberry is completely crushed and there are no large pieces left.

8 Strain the strawberry pulp and extraction into a medium glass container.

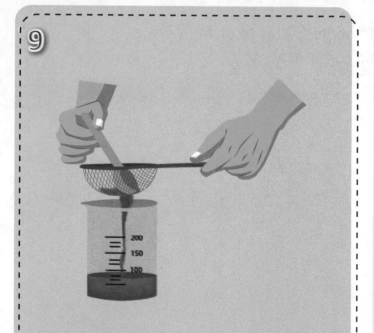

9 Using a spoon, press the strawberry pulp against the strainer, so that more of the mixture is collected in the container.

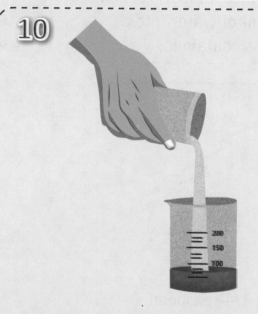

10 Now, pour the extraction mixture you just strained into a smaller glass container. This is done to isolate the DNA on the surface of the mixture.

11

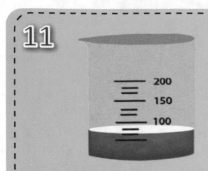

Next, add 1 teaspoon of chilled isopropyl alcohol to the solution. Hold the container at eye level. You should see a white layer on top of the mixture.

12

Using tweezers, gently remove the white mixture from the solution and lay it on a dish to examine under a microscope. It is the DNA of the strawberry.

The STEM behind it

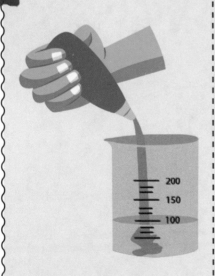

When we add soap to this process, it helps to dissolve the cell membranes of the strawberry.

Adding salt to the mixture breaks up the protein chains in the strawberry and releases the DNA strands.

The ice-cold isopropyl alcohol does not dissolve the DNA, which helps us to separate it from the mixture.

QUICKSAND

Life Connect : Quicksand

DIFFICULTY LEVEL

Adult supervision required

You Need
- 450 g of cornstarch
- Water
- Food coloring
- A large bowl
- A stirring spoon
- A ziplock bag

1

Add about 150 g of cornstarch into a large bowl. Pour around 350 ml water into a plastic cup and add few drops of food coloring to it. Stir it with a spoon to mix the color evenly.

2

Now, slowly, add 1/2 cup of water to the bowl. Mix the water and cornstarch with your hand until both ingredients are blended.

3

If the mixture seems dry, add more water to the bowl in small amounts until it reaches a consistency such that it should be thick, easy to stir, and flow like a liquid. The quicksand is ready.

4 Put your hand into the mixture. Can you move your hand quickly? No! If you grab the quicksand and pull it up, it would feel as if your hand is sinking.

The STEM behind it

Quicksand sometimes feels like a solid and sometimes like a liquid.

Cornstarch is made up of particles that are cross-linked with each other. On poking the quicksand hard and fast, the particles become entangled, making it harder to flow.

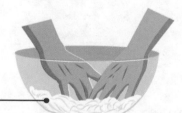

However, when we poke it gently, it acts like a liquid because the particles of cornstarch have enough space to move around each other.

99

LET'S MEASURE EARTH'S CIRCUMFERENCE

Life Connect: Measurement

DIFFICULTY LEVEL

Adult supervision required

You Need

- A flat, level ground in direct sunlight
- A meterstick
- A pencil
- A calculator
- A protractor
- A long piece of string
- A bucket or flower pot
- Soil
- An adult helper

1 Fill a bucket or flower pot with soil to the top. Set up a meterstick vertically in the bucket so that it stays upright.

2 At solar noon, mark the end of the meterstick's shadow on the ground.

3 Have an adult stretch a piece of string between the top of the meterstick and the end of its shadow.

4 Using a protractor, measure the angle between the string and the meterstick in degrees. Note the measurement. Now, calculate the distance between your city and the equator.

5 To conclude, calculate the circumference of the Earth using this equation: Circumference = 360 x distance between your city and the equator/angle of shadow that you measured.

The STEM behind it

This method was used by Eratosthenes, a Greek mathematician, around 2,200 years ago. He measured the angle of a shadow cast by a tall object in Alexandria. Using geometry, he calculated the circumference of the Earth based on the following information:

- There are 360° in a circle.
- The measure of the angle of the shadow cast by a tall object in Alexandria.
- The overland distance between Alexandria and Syene.

The resulting equation was:

Angle of shadow in Alexandria/360° = Distance between Alexandria and Syene/Circumference of the Earth.

WALKING HORSE

Life Connect: Potential energy, kinetic energy and gravity

DIFFICULTY LEVEL

1

Using a ruler, draw a 15x4.5 cm rectangle on the card stock.

2

5 CM	5 CM	5 CM
LEG		LEG
HEAD	1.5 cm 1.5 cm 1.5 cm	TAIL
LEG		LEG

↑.03 CM

Divide the rectangle into different sections, using the same dimension as shown here. This is the template for your paper horse.

3

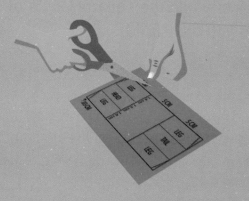

Now, cut the rectangle around its perimeter. Then, carefully cut along the dotted lines inside the rectangle and the small diagonal lines along the corners.

4

Bend the legs, i.e., all the four outer rectangles of the horse so that they are perpendicular to the body, which is, the middle square.

5 Curl the tail of the horse using a pencil.

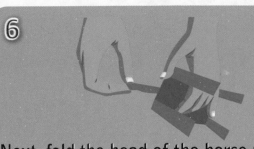

6 Next, fold the head of the horse up. Then, fold about an inch of the head down to shape it into a triangle.

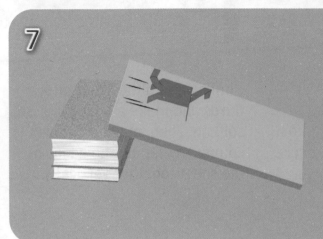

7 Stack a few books and place a chopping board on them. Now, place the paper horse on the chopping board as shown. Give the horse a little push. The horse walks down the board.

The STEM behind it

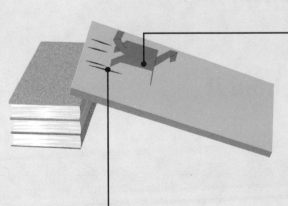

When we place the paper horse on the books and chopping board arrangement, it gains more potential energy because of being at a height.

When we push the horse, it is pulled down the board due to gravity due to which potential energy changes into kinetic energy.

This kinetic energy makes the horse wobble back and forth, gaining momentum as it moves.

101

WHICH SHAPE IS THE STRONGEST?

Life Connect: Strength of structures

DIFFICULTY LEVEL

You Need
- Three to four sheets of paper
- Several notebooks of the same size
- Scissors
- Tape

1

Fold a sheet of paper into half. Fold the paper into half again such that the paper has four even segments.

2

Now, fold the paper into a square column and secure its edges with tape.

3

Similarly, fold the sheet into thirds and make a triangular column. Then, make a circular column, by taping the edges of the sheet together vertically.

4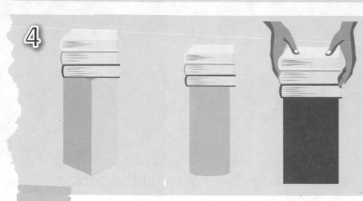

Stand each column up on a table. Carefully place a number of notebooks on top of each column. Make sure the size and number of notebooks is the same on all the columns. Which column holds the maximum number of books? It is the circular column.

The STEM behind it

The circular column holds the maximum number of notebooks because it doesn't have any edges. The weight of the notebooks is evenly distributed, that is, all parts of the circular column are sharing the load of the notebooks and contribute to its overall strength.

The square and triangular columns have edges and corners. The weight of the notebooks is shifted to its edges and corners which deform easily, and as a result of this the columns collapse.